CAMBRIDGE
UNIVERSITY PRESS

Shaftesbury Road, Cambridge CB2 8EA, United Kingdom

One Liberty Plaza, 20th Floor, New York, NY 10006, USA

477 Williamstown Road, Port Melbourne, VIC 3207, Australia

314–321, 3rd Floor, Plot 3, Splendor Forum, Jasola District Centre, New Delhi – 110025, India

103 Penang Road, #05–06/07, Visioncrest Commercial, Singapore 238467

Cambridge University Press is part of Cambridge University Press & Assessment, a department of the University of Cambridge.

We share the University's mission to contribute to society through the pursuit of education, learning and research at the highest international levels of excellence.

www.cambridge.org
Information on this title: www.cambridge.org/9781009113366

DOI: 10.1017/9781009119658

© Helen Young and Kavita Mudan Finn 2022

First published 2022

A catalogue record for this publication is available from the British Library.

ISBN 978-1-009-11336-6 Paperback
ISSN 2632-3427 (online)
ISSN 2632-3419 (print)

Cambridge Elements ≡

Elements in the Global Middle Ages
edited by
Geraldine Heng
University of Texas at Austin
Susan Noakes
University of Minnesota, Twin Cities

GLOBAL MEDIEVALISM

An Introduction

Helen Young
Deakin University

Kavita Mudan Finn
Independent Scholar

CAMBRIDGE
UNIVERSITY PRESS

Global Medievalism

An Introduction

Elements in the Global Middle Ages

DOI: 10.1017/9781009119658
First published online: September 2022

Helen Young
Deakin University

Kavita Mudan Finn
Independent Scholar

Author for correspondence: Kavita Mudan Finn, kvmfinn@gmail.com

Abstract: The typical vision of the Middle Ages that Western popular culture represents to its global audience is deeply Eurocentric. *The Lord of the Rings* and *Game of Thrones* franchises imagine entire medievalist worlds, but we see only a fraction of them through the stories and travels of the characters. Organised around the theme of mobility, this Element seeks to deconstruct the Eurocentric orientations of Western popular medievalisms, which typically position Europe as either the whole world or the centre of it, by making them visible and offering alternative perspectives. How does popular culture represent medievalist worlds as global – connected by the movement of people and objects? How do imagined mobilities allow us to create counterstories that resist Eurocentric norms? This study represents the start of what will hopefully be a fruitful and inclusive conversation about what the Middle Ages did and should look like.

Keywords: medieval, popular culture, medievalism, fantasy, Vikings

ISBNs: 9781009113366 (PB), 9781009119658 (OC)
ISSNs: 2632-3427 (online), 2632-3419 (print)

Contents

Introduction

Medievalism, the reimagining and repurposing of the Middle Ages, is a staple of twenty-first-century political and popular culture. Arguably all popular culture medievalisms are political because popular culture both reflects and shapes the ideologies of its production including, although not uniquely, models for identification and in-group/out-group divisions. Like academic medieval studies, popular culture medievalism conventionally 'desires and reifies a white, predominately cisgender and male, Middle Ages'.[1] The association of medieval Europe and the people who lived there with whiteness, and their position as holders of white heritage, are rooted not in historical evidence, but in a reimagined history that selectively interprets known – and imagined – people and events in the service of modern racist ideologies, nationalism, colonialism, and imperialism. White Western medievalism tells and retells in new modes and media a story about the past that justifies present oppressive structures as natural, inevitable, and right; as Dorothy Kim warns, 'medieval studies is intimately entwined with white supremacy and has been so for a long time'.[2] Counterstories can and must be told to resist the oppression and violence habitually storied into medievalism, not least through its adoption by fascistic white extremists to, as Mary Rambaran-Olm, Bree Leake, and Micah James Goodrich put it, 'protect each other and the futures that we imagine'.[3] We enter this Element in a spirit of radical hope, seeking to deconstruct white Western popular medievalisms and to identify and promote strategies of counterstorytelling. We start, then, with the emerging critical orientation in medieval studies that organises this series: the global Middle Ages.

What Are the Global Middle Ages?

We pose this question in the present tense because 'the Middle Ages' were invented after the fact and have in some sense been continually reinvented ever since. The Middle Ages of 2022 are not the Middle Ages of 2002 any more than they were the Middle Ages of 1602. These processes of reinvention – that is, medievalism – have produced multiple, often conflicting, 'Middle Ages': sites of barbarism that are also objects of nostalgia – violent, muddy, and bloody but also courtly, chivalric, and romantic.[4]

---

[1] Rambaran-Olm, Leake, and Goodrich, 'Medieval Studies', 357.
[2] Kim, 'Teaching Medieval Studies in a Time of White Supremacy'.
[3] Rambaran-Olm, Leake, and Goodrich, 'Medieval Studies', 357.
[4] Eco, *Travels in Hyperreality*, 61–85. See also David Matthews' discussion of grotesque and romantic medievalism in *Medievalism*, 15.

The European Middle Ages were created by fifteenth-century Italian human-ists to delineate the millennium or so between their own time and the end of the classical period that they claimed to be reinvigorating in a renaissance. The medieval is first and foremost a temporal construct: a time between times, a kind of limbo, and its existence demands a fundamental division between pre-modern and modern. As Geraldine Heng and Lynn Ramey argue: 'Time in the West sees modernity as a unique and singular arrival that ends the long eras of premodernity, instantiating the origin of new, never-before phenomena: the Scientific Revolution, the Industrial Revolution, the beginnings of colonization, empire, race, et alia.'[5]

According to this story, only the West became modern – with all that modernity entails – at the right time. This reimagined temporality enabled colonialism and imperialism by positioning every non-European people and culture as pre-modern, backward, and uncivilised and therefore in 'need' of European civilisation. Thus too begins the myth of 'progress' with which we grapple to this day in the Global North and West.

In this story the Middle Ages are bounded not only by time but also by space – they happen only in Europe. The turn towards medievalism as a favoured paradigm of identity formation in Europe was driven by ethnona-tionalisms; it 'could be imagined as bottom-up and organic, to be found in the blood, the soil, the language, and the material remains of one's own place'.[6] As Sharon Kinoshita observes, however, 'the nationalist paradigms that have traditionally shaped our understanding of the Middle Ages are frequently ill-suited to the objects they purport to explain' because the borders of people, nation, and language use shifted during both the medieval and modern eras.[7] Events like the Danish and Norman conquests of England are retrospectively framed as intra-racial amalgamations of Germanic (or Gothic) peoples as early as the sixteenth-century writings of Richard Verstegan and William Camden. This belief in the immobility of populations – in this case, for an entire millennium – is fundamental to the construction of white supremacy. It is imagined as having been long enough that various subgroups within that category of *Homo europaeus* (white man), such as Goths, Celts, Anglo-Saxons, and so forth, distilled their specific racial characteristics and expressed them through divergent cultures and social institutions. This story of a distinct European spatio-temporality that crystalises white identities to the exclusion of all others is critical to European colonialism and imperialism

---

[5] Heng and Ramey, 'Early Globalities, Global Literatures', 391.
[6] D'Arcens and Lynch, 'Introduction', xiii–xiv. On medievalism and the formation of modern European nations, see, for example, Geary, *The Myth of Nations*.
[7] Kinoshita, *Medieval Boundaries*, 3.

and is deeply entangled with contemporary popular culture medievalisms. But it is not the only story that can be told. The Middle Ages can – and should – be global.

This Element follows Geraldine Heng's foundational theorisation of a 'global Middle Ages' as one that decentres Europe, disrupts European temporalities, and deconstructs the raced spatio-temporality of 'medieval'.[8] As Heng and Ramey argue, it does this by producing 'the recognition that *modernity itself* is a repeating transhistorical phenomenon, with a footprint in different vectors of the world moving at different rates of speed'.[9] Furthermore, the 'pure' white medieval Europe of the contemporary Western imagination is a creation of modernity generated through and by centuries of retellings, and it is rooted in a rhetoric of ethnonationalism and colonialist fantasy. The global Middle Ages should instead be considered a framework for counterstorying the European Middle Ages, one which disrupts structures and reveals omissions and contradictions while offering a more expansive, complex, and ethical narrative of the past. Decolonising the Middle Ages by decentring Europe and disrupting white colonialist spatio-temporal narratives is in no way limited to academia. The Black Museum's *Caravans of Gold: Fragments in Time* exhibition in 2019, for example, explored Saharan trade and its interconnections of West Africa, North Africa, the Middle East, and Europe from the eighth to the sixteenth centuries. A similar concept informs the work of the J. Paul Getty Museum.[10] We reject the application of a 'global Middle Ages' label as an anodyne 'diversity initiative' of a field that remains steeped in the white heteropatriarchal colonialism that Sierra Lomuto has powerfully critiqued.[11] In order to do this, we follow 'Margo Hendricks' intersectional framework of premodern critical race studies, which 'recognizes the capacity of the analytical gaze to define the premodern as a multiethnic system of competing sovereignties'.[12] While the material we analyse often presents a white- or Eurocentric perspective, it is our goal to interrogate that perspective and, where possible, to offer counterstories. When we speak, then, of the global Middle Ages we mean the epistemological, political, and medievalist project that seeks to tell new stories about the medieval past and what we can do with it in the present – including the futures we can imagine through it. We acknowledge our own positions as a white person in the Global South (Helen) and a South Asian woman in the Global North (Kavita),

---

[8] See, for example, Heng, 'The Global Middle Ages' and 'Early Globalities, and Its Questions, Objectives, and Methods'.

[9] Heng and Ramey, 'Early Globalities, Global Literatures', 391.

[10] Berzock, *Caravans of Gold, Fragments in Time*. For the Getty project, see Keene, *Toward a Global Middle Ages*.

[11] Lomuto, 'Becoming Postmedieval'.

[12] Hendricks, 'Coloring the Past, Considerations on Our Future', 379.

both with scholarly roots in anglophone literature, and we have made efforts to expand our citational genealogies to better reflect what the global Middle Ages should look like; any errors or omissions are our own.

What Is Global Medievalism?

Medievalism is a process of storytelling even when it lacks a conventional narrative element. Neo-Gothic cathedrals in settler colonial states like Australia, Canada, or the United States, for example, tell a story about white European possession of the land. Like culture as a whole, medievalism is 'concerned with meanings, pleasures and identities'.[13] We may think of it, then, as an ongoing process of storytelling that manages what meanings are attached to 'the Middle Ages' and therefore also manages who can take pleasure in and construct identities through that imagined past. In its present form it has principally told a story of the bounded European Middle Ages that centres Europe and whiteness (in its multiple formations) to the degree that they have been made synonymous. This is not to say that only white people can enjoy or do identity work through medievalism; black and anti-racist medievalisms have existed for centuries, as scholarship from Matthew X. Vernon, Jonathan Hsy, and others increasingly shows.[14] Nonetheless white people have privileged access to medievalist stories, and most Western popular culture reiterates centuries of medievalisms that have contributed to, justified, and upheld white power and ideologies.

Medievalism is deeply linked to European imperial and colonial projects and to the white racial formations that underlie them. An originally Eurocentric concept, 'the Middle Ages' were taken to other parts of the world, where they served imperialist ideologies to colonisers and colonised alike.[15] It had always already positioned the 'rest' of the world as backward, deficient, and not just open to but in need of European domination. Candace Barrington argues that global medievalism is a colonialist process that asserts and reasserts white heteropatriarchal power and possession in that it 'uses the European medieval past as prism for interpreting, shaping, and binding cultures outside the Western European nation-states'.[16] While we contest Barrington's exact terminology here – preferring the critical conceptualisation of 'global' explained earlier in

---

[13] Fiske, *Understanding Popular Culture*, 1.

[14] Hsy, *Antiracist Medievalisms*; Vernon, *The Black Middle Ages*; Davis and Altschul, *Medievalisms and the Postcolonial World*.

[15] For example, Altschul, *Geographies of Philological Knowledge*; D'Arcens, Lynch, and Trigg, 'Medievalism, Nationalism, Colonialism'; D'Arcens, *Old Songs in the Timeless Land*; Davis, *Periodization and Sovereignty*; Warren, *Creole Medievalism*.

[16] Barrington, 'Global Medievalism and Translation', 183. On white colonial possession-taking, see Moreton-Robinson, *The White Possessive*.

this Element – she nonetheless offers a typology of medievalisms – spatial, temporal, and linguistic – that is useful for understanding white Western medievalism and highlighting the potential for post- and decolonial medievalisms that resist those norms.[17]

Temporal medievalism takes place when non-Western peoples and cultures (colonised or not) are positioned as 'medieval' and therefore uncivilised by modern European cultures.[18] Predicated on a strict divide between medieval and modern, temporal medievalism is used in European nations and settler colonies to marginalise and belittle peoples and their cultures who are positioned as 'non-white' in any particular context. Spatial medievalism sees settler colonies like Australia and the USA invest in the Middle Ages as part of their national heritage and enables people outside Europe to engage in temporal medievalism.[19] As Adam Miyashiro argues, in white 'heritage politics' of nations like the USA and Australia, 'the settler colonial project is not critiqued but lauded as an extension of medieval Europe'.[20] Linguistic medievalism, however, is a resistant, 'counter', or postcolonial mode that sees colonised cultures 'appropriate colonial medieval texts for their own purposes'.[21] Tracy Banivanua-Mar argues that one type of decolonisation is 'a dialogue that Indigenous peoples maintained with colonial powers, and in which they asserted their right to choose the best and reject the worst of colonisation'.[22] Taking our cues from this insight, we propose that global medievalism chooses what suits its purpose from the colonialist 'medieval' and rejects what does not – either by refusing to engage with it or by reconfiguring it. It thus produces a new, resistant counterstory that disrupts white colonial and imperialist logics of hegemonic medievalisms.

Global medievalism is the process of telling the stories of a global Middle Ages, a form of critical race counterstorytelling that is committed to undoing the storying of the 'European Middle Ages' and to generating new stories about the past and, through them, the present and future. Medievalism is always about the present and points towards the future even as it reimagines the past. Stories about the past imply a future even when they do not represent it. Global medievalism, then, imagines a past that could lead to a more equitable, just,

---

[17] For example, Davis and Altschul, *Medievalisms and the Postcolonial World*; Altschul, 'Medievalism and the Contemporaneity of the Medieval in Postcolonial Brazil'; Lampert-Weissig, *Medieval Literature and Postcolonial Studies*, 108–50; Karkov, Kłosowska, and Oei, *Disturbing Times*; Ellard, 'Historical Hauntings'.

[18] Barrington, 'Global Medievalism and Translation', 183.

[19] Barrington, 'Global Medievalism and Translation', 187–9.

[20] Miyashiro, 'Our Deeper Past', 4.

[21] Barrington, 'Global Medievalism and Translation', 190.

[22] Banivanua Mar, *Decolonisation and the Pacific*, 4.

and inclusive future where present oppressive power structures (capitalist colonialist white heteropatriarchy) can be dismantled or, in fantasy worlds, were never allowed to exist. The received medieval past is powerful but can be resisted through counterstorytelling. This can involve, for example, telling medievalist stories from subaltern perspectives, deconstructing myths of the European Middle Ages, centring people and cultures from parts of the world that are not Europe, and emphasising global connections. Global medievalism dovetails with Louise D'Arcens' helpful formulation of 'world medievalism' in that both are transhistorical, transnational, and transcultural.[23] We prefer the term 'global' for its connections with the critical 'global Middle Ages' discussed earlier in this Element, and because our interest here is specifically in medievalisms that resist colonialist capitalism associated with modern globality. In this Element we argue that global medievalism manifests in twenty-first-century popular culture through an exploration of stories and counterstories in that domain. Counterstories to white Western medievalisms have a centuries-old history; we ask how they manifest in contemporary popular culture and look forward to many more to come.

Popular Culture and Global Medievalism

There is no simple and generally agreed-on definition of popular culture. Imre Szeman and Susie O'Brien offer a useful outline: 'entertainment produced through and by commercial media (television, film, the music industry, etc.) that have the economic and technological capacity to reach large, demographically diverse, and geographically dispersed audiences'.[24] This provides an ideal focus here for two reasons: it encompasses the transnational nature of much of contemporary popular culture, and commercial entertainment media is one of the key sites of medievalism in the twenty-first century (and earlier).[25] The features of popular culture as defined here emerge variously in the texts we explore in later sections. These range from vast multimedia franchises such as that built around J. R. R. Tolkien's *Lord of the Rings* or George R. R. Martin's *A Song of Ice and Fire* novels, to fantasy and historical fiction novels from multinational publishing houses and small presses.

---

[23] D'Arcens prefers 'world' to 'global', arguing that, as a term, it is 'a more amenable concept for a cultural phenomenon such as medievalism: it exceeds the global in its temporal depth and horizon, accommodating an idea of transcultural ecumene that reaches back beyond the period when 'globe' became synonymous with global capitalism'. *World Medievalism*, 16.

[24] Szeman and O'Brien, *Popular Culture*, 24.

[25] In scholarship of popular culture, 'global' is typically used in a colloquial sense meaning multi- or transnational, or in relation to modern globalisation (e.g. Crother, *Globalization and American Popular Culture*).

Early studies of popular medievalisms often focussed on film,[26] but interest has grown exponentially in the past decade or so, resulting in a vastly expanded scope of reference and substantial theorisation.[27] Some scholars in medievalism studies have dismissed popular culture medievalism because of a perceived lack of interest in the historical Middle Ages.[28] Others have appropriated Umberto Eco's derogatory term 'neomedievalism' in theorisations of how popular (especially electronic) medievalisms function, often by seeking differences from other kinds of medievalism.[29] High, public history, and popular medievalisms have all substantially contributed to the construction of a European rather than a global Middle Ages.[30] Recent scholarship on Anglo-Saxonism demonstrates this further.[31] Popular culture medievalisms use their own logics and values when it comes to balancing commercial, recreational, and educational priorities. They may have different formal features, strategies, and plots to other medievalisms, but they habitually tell the same story of the European Middle Ages. We therefore prefer the expansive 'medievalism' over variations such as 'neomedieval'.

Popular culture shapes what we 'know' about the Middle Ages[32] and is part of the mass media ecosystem that circulates political medievalisms attached to contemporary ideologies.[33] The dominant mode of twenty-first-century popular medievalism is the 'gritty' or 'grimdark' approach associated with the *Game of Thrones* and *Witcher* franchises, which reinscribes white racial medievalisms even as it asserts its own difference from Tolkien and Disney films.[34] Genre and subgenre are important considerations because they shape both production and reception, ultimately impacting what is understood to be the historically authentic representation of the medieval past.[35] It would be easy to dismiss popular culture medievalisms as merely subject to hegemonic power. As bell hooks

[26] For example, Harty, *The Reel Middle Ages*; Driver and Ray, *The Medieval Hero on Screen*.
[27] D'Arcens and Lynch, *International Medievalism and Popular Culture*; Marshall, *Mass Market Medieval*; Young (ed.), *Fantasy and Science Fiction Medievalisms*; Young (ed.), *The Middle Ages in Popular Culture*.
[28] Alexander, *Medievalism*; Eco, *Travels in Hyperreality*.
[29] Fitzpatrick, *Neomedievalism*; Marshall, 'Neomedievalism, Identification, and the Haze of Medievalism'; Utz, 'A Moveable Feast'. The journal *Studies in Medievalism* has hosted much of the theoretical discussion, especially in themed volumes XIX and XX in 2010 and 2011.
[30] Young, 'Place and Time'; Young, *Race and Popular Fantasy Literature*, 15–87; Mitchell-Smith, 'The United Princesses of America'; Fimi, *Tolkien, Race, and Cultural History*; Cecire, 'Medievalism, Popular Culture and National Identity in Children's Fantasy Literature'; Rambaran-Olm, 'Sounds about White'.
[31] Ellard, *Anglo-Saxon(ist) Pasts, postSaxon Futures*; Miyashiro, 'Decolonizing Anglo-Saxon Studies'; Miyashiro, '"Our Deeper Past"'; Rambaran-Olm, 'Anglo-Saxon Studies, Academia and White Supremacy'; Wilton, 'What Do We Mean by *Anglo-Saxon*?'
[32] Sturtevant, 'Based on a True History?'   [33] Elliott, *Medievalism, Politics and Mass Media*.
[34] Young, *Race and Popular Fantasy Literature*, 63–87.
[35] Elliott, *Remaking the Middle Ages*, 215–16.

argues, however, 'when we desire to decolonize minds and imaginations …
popular culture can be and is a powerful site for intervention, challenge, and
change'.[36] Building on this idea is the work of Ebony Elizabeth Thomas, who
argues that 'restorying' can transform even multinational franchises into sites of
emancipatory resistance to the hegemonies that medievalism conventionally
upholds.[37]

Barrington's typology of white colonial and resistant medievalisms, outlined
earlier in this Element, is a useful starting point to explore different ways
popular culture medievalisms work and how they might be global. Temporal
medievalism – the positioning of others as medieval and therefore backward
and uncivilised compared to the modern white Western self – takes a slightly
different form in popular culture. When the narrative present is coded as
European medieval, temporal medievalism positions others as not yet or not
even medieval; we see this Orientalist framework on full display in HBO's
Game of Thrones (2011–19) and the BBC's *The Last Kingdom* (2015–20).[38]
Audiences in settler colonies like Australia and the USA engage in spatial
medievalism when they understand the medievalist narrative present of these
programmes as being connected to their heritage. J. R. R. Tolkien's *The Lord of
the Rings* offers an illustrative example of how temporal and spatial medievalism contribute to the story of a 'European Middle Ages' through popular
culture.

While the phrase never appears in his published writings, Tolkien is often
said to have created a mythology for England.[39] His was not a purely nationalist
medievalism, however; while he spent most of his life in England, he was
actually born in the colony of South Africa. His medievalism was profoundly
white, racial, and Eurocentric[40] with substantial Germanic and Anglo-Saxonist
elements; he praised the 'noble Northern spirit' that he believed characterised
white Germanic people, including the English, and those English who partici-
pated in the colonial project.[41] His own devotion to medieval English language
and literature illustrates this. *The Lord of the Rings*, moreover, models spatial

---

[36] hooks, *Outlaw Culture*, 5.   [37] Thomas, *The Dark Fantastic*, 159–64.
[38] See Downes and Young, 'The Maiden Fair'; Hardy, 'The East Is Least'. We discuss *Game of Thrones* later in this Element.
[39] For a discussion of Tolkien's ethnonationalism, see Fimi, *Tolkien, Race and Cultural History*
[40] Fimi, *Tolkien, Race, and Cultural History*; Young, *Race and Popular Fantasy Literature*, 15–39; Lavezzo, 'Whiteness, Medievalism, Immigration'; Young, 'Diversity and Difference'. The *Rings of Power* television series has not yet aired at the time of this writing, but advance publicity has indicated a more racially diverse approach to casting than prior Tolkien adaptations.
[41] Balfe, 'Incredible Geographies?'; Firchow, 'The Politics of Fantasy'; Obertino, 'Barbarians and Imperialism in Tacitus and *The Lord of the Rings*'; Shippey, *The Road to Middle Earth*, 152. For Anglo-Saxonism, see Horsman, *Race and Manifest Destiny*.

medievalism through the relationship of the colonial kingdom of Gondor to the fallen realm of Numenor. The people of Gondor are 'the race of Numenor' while, when Aragorn is crowned, he repeats the words of his Numenorean colonising ancestor: 'Out of the Great Sea to Middle-earth I am come. In this place will I abide, and my heirs, unto the ending of the world.'[42] Spatial medievalism is also significantly at play in the reception of *The Lord of the Rings* in settler colonies; indeed, a significant tourist industry has emerged following the filming of Peter Jackson's two Tolkien trilogies in Aeotearoa (New Zealand) that conflates real-world locations with parts of Middle-earth.[43]

Temporal medievalism in a colonialist mode is clear in the encounter of the Riders of Rohan with the 'Wild-Men' of the Druadan Forest. Their leader, Ghan-buri-Ghan, is introduced as part of nature rather than human: 'a strange squat shape of a man, gnarled as an old stone ... clad only with grass around his waist'.[44] The hobbit Merry sees a resemblance to ancient statues in Rohan: 'here was one of those old images, brought to life, or maybe a creature descended in true line through the endless years from the models used by the forgotten craftsmen long ago'.[45] In exchange for passage through the forest, they ask the Rohirrim to 'drive away bad dark with bright iron' so that 'Wild Men can go back to sleep in the wild woods'.[46] Afterwards they vanish, 'never to be seen by any Rider of Rohan again'.[47] Ghan-buri-Ghan and his people are first constructed as existing out of time, backwards, and uncivilised compared to the 'medieval' Rohirrim and Gondorians and so unable and unwilling to change that they disappear from the narrative and the implied future of Middle-earth. Thus even texts with a medieval narrative present utilise modes of exclusion to position people outside the temporality that leads to implied modernity.

Colonialist spatial and temporal medievalisms have marginalised Indigenous peoples through discourses that are, as the aforementioned example demonstrates, significant in popular culture. As we worked on this Element, Helen described the project to Professor Daniel Heath Justice, a Cherokee man, Indigenous studies scholar, and author of speculative fictions. He nodded along enthusiastically until the word 'medievalism' was mentioned. The colonialist entanglements of medievalism have specifically functioned to exclude Indigenous peoples for so long – and are themselves so profound – that this is not surprising. Global medievalism raises the prospect, but the hegemonic power of multinational popular culture, often aligned with neocolonialism, weighs against its realisation. Justice recommended to us the only global

---

[42] Tolkien, *Return of the King*, 1268.
[43] For fan tourism, see Williams, 'Fan Tourism and Pilgrimage'.
[44] Tolkien, *Return of the King*, 1088.   [45] Tolkien, *Return of the King*, 1088.
[46] Tolkien, *Return of the King*, 1089.   [47] Tolkien, *Return of the King*, 1092.

medievalist popular culture work by Indigenous creators that we have been able to identify: the young adult historical novel *Skraelings: Clashes in the Old Arctic* (2014) by Rachel Qitsualik-Tinsley and Sean Qitsualik-Tinsley, who are of Inuit heritage.[48] We discuss it in detail in the next section. Nonetheless global medievalism is part of contemporary popular culture, and we explore its various manifestations in the subsequent three sections.

Mobilities and Global Medievalism

Mobilities are our central concept for 'grasping the global' in popular culture medievalism in this Element.[49] Contemporary studies of mobility, which are grounded in the social sciences, focus on the movement of objects, people, money, and ideas, individually and en masse, on local, national, and international scales.[50] We draw on Heng's usage as one of three foundational trajectories of global Middle Ages approaches. '[O]ne is focused on mobilities: how people, ideas, material objects, technologies, and cultures crisscrossed the planet. Another is centered on points of anchoring or mooring: the cities and states, trading blocs and ports at which the world met and transacted, and where human relations bloomed.'[51] The third trajectory is 'fixed on time: continuity and change, the interanimation of past and present', and thus on the movements of people, objects, and concepts through time.[52] This suggests to us not only the interplay of temporalities that a global view produces, but also the temporal movement inherent in popular medievalisms that re-present the medieval in modernity for us to watch, read, and play. In this Element we add 'temporal' to the dimensions of mobilities.

Attention to mobilities in all their forms reveals social and cultural systems, structures, and power relations: '[M]obility and control over mobility both reflect and reinforce power. Mobility is a resource to which not everyone has an equal relationship.'[53] Mobility can be an indication of power or the lack thereof in cases of invasion and forced displacement, two modes integral to colonialism. The modes and manifestations of mobilities, then, can reveal not only the power structures of fictional worlds, but the medievalisms that underpin those worlds, global or not. Who and what travels, and why? Where from

---

[48] This is not to suggest that there are no Indigenous medievalisms; rather, we are observing here a specific site of exclusion within popular culture. On Indigenous studies and medieval studies in academic medievalism, see Andrews, 'Indigenous Futures and Medieval Pasts'. See also Yim, 'Reading Hawaiian Shakespeare'.

[49] Ong, *Neoliberalism As Exception*, 121.

[50] See, for example, Sheller and Urry, 'The New Mobilities Paradigm'; Hannam, Sheller, and Urry, Mobilities, Immobilities and Moorings'.

[51] Heng, 'Romancing the Portal', 44.   [52] Heng, 'Romancing the Portal', 44.

[53] Skeggs, *Class, Self, Culture*, 49.

and to? What power structures are revealed by exploring these questions? Is there a centre where all roads lead? What patterns of mobilities and moorings characterise the spatial and temporal medievalisms of contemporary popular culture, drawing them into the hegemonic Western story of the European Middle Ages? What patterns of moorings and mobilities characterise the counterstorytelling of global medievalism?

In the next section we explore representations of Vikings, who were among the great medieval travellers, in two twenty-first-century historical fictions: the television series *Vikings* (2013–20) and the young adult novel *Skraelings* (2014), mentioned earlier. Vikings, and Norse people more generally, were folded into white racial medievalisms from the second half of the eighteenth century, and narratives about them – fictional and otherwise – were part of the storying of the European Middle Ages in national and colonial projects in the nineteenth and twentieth centuries. We argue that mobilities and moorings in *Vikings* are mapped onto those of earlier centuries and show that spatial and temporal medievalisms are at play throughout its six seasons. *Skraelings* counters these stories with its global medievalism, decentring the Vikings and putting their brief presence in medieval north America to the purposes of Indigenous people there.

We then turn to epic fantasy to analyse how medievalisms shape imaginary worlds. The Eurocentric conventions of medievalist fantasy connect imagined worlds not with realities of any historical Middle Ages, but with centuries of spatial and temporal medievalist storytelling. Our two central case studies are the franchise built around George R. R. Martin's unfinished book series *A Song of Ice and Fire* (1996–) and Samantha Shannon's *The Priory of the Orange Tree* (2019). We explore the journeys of key characters through imagined cultural geographies that are broadly analogous to those of the real world and use Ulrich Beck's theorisation of 'world-risk society' to develop our argument for the capacity of popular culture to produce global medievalism.[54] Genre conventions that reproduce spatial and temporal medievalisms can, through processes of counterstorytelling, be deconstructed and rebuilt through global medievalism.

Fantasy, arguably the most prominent genre of popular medievalism in the twenty-first century, is also the focus of the next section, which offers two modes for constructively engaging with the global Middle Ages. The first, exemplified in Shannon A. Chakraborty's Daevabad Trilogy, decentres the narrative from Europe entirely, focussing on an imagined world anchored in Islam and Middle Eastern history. Rather than playing into harmful

---

[54] Beck, *World Risk Society.*

Islamophobic stereotypes, as so often happens in medievalist (and, indeed, medieval) texts, Chakraborty's narrative offers a compelling corrective, and, through its use of mobilities for its central characters, illuminates the fascinating medieval network in and around the Indian Ocean. The second mode is that of deconstruction, the transformation of an existing canonical European narrative – in this case, the imagined universe of the Arthurian legend – and its restorying from a new perspective in novel and short story form. Given the scope of the topic, we cannot hope to be remotely exhaustive, but our goal in this Element is to start a conversation, to plant the seeds of stories yet to come.

Medieval Mobilities: Vikings

If there is any icon of medieval mobility in contemporary popular culture it is the Viking longship. It was referred to as 'the Internet of the year 1000, connecting places and people who themselves could not even imagine what lay beyond the wide sea or that mountain range' by then First Lady Hillary Rodham Clinton, in the catalogue for the Smithsonian exhibition, *Vikings: The North Atlantic Saga* in 2000.[55] Clinton describes Vikings as 'explorers' and 'among the earliest conveyors of information and experience and culture between one place and another'.[56] While Viking mobility was significant and enabled mobilities of other people, culture, ideas, and objects, the suggestion that they were 'among the earliest' humans to do this ignores millennia of history and problematically resonates with discourses of white racial exceptionalism. Historically, Vikings travelled at least as far as the littoral of the North American continent in the west and to Baghdad and the Caspian Sea in the east, and the trading networks they connected with stretched further along the Silk Roads into Asia. Paying attention to historical Viking travels highlights the globality of the medieval world and mobilities of people and goods within it.

Vikings reimagined in popular culture might be reasonably expected to highlight the globality of medieval Europe given their significant mobility. This potential, however, is rarely realised. Modern reimaginings of Vikings are closely tied to white national and transnational medievalisms and have been since at least the eighteenth century.[57] In this section we explore how Viking mobilities – including those of non-Norse people, and the trade in goods and money they enabled – are represented in popular culture. We begin by arguing that the Vikings, enemies of the English for some three hundred

---

[55] Clinton, 'Preface', 10.   [56] Clinton, 'Preface', 10.
[57] Clunies Ross, *The Norse Muse in Britain*; Young, 'Thomas Percy's Racialization of the European Middle Ages'.

years of the medieval period, were appropriated as part of English and settler colonial identities through a process of spatial medievalism that helped construct transnational white Germanic identity. This story of white Western identity is retold in contemporary popular culture through the analysis of the History Channel television programme *Vikings* (2013–20). While counterstorying of Vikings is almost non-existent in Western popular culture, *Skraelings* (2014) by Inuit authors Rachel and Sean Qitsualik-Tinsley demonstrates the potential for global medievalism to profoundly reimagine their significance.

Norse Culture, Whiteness, and Spatial Medievalism

In order to understand the significance of Norse people, society, and culture, Vikings in particular, and their representation in contemporary popular, culture requires us to go back to the 'medieval turn' in Europe in the second half of the eighteenth century.[58] From the sixteenth century onward, in an effort to differentiate themselves from earlier generations, European intellectuals had looked to classical Greece and Rome as exemplars. The turn towards medievalism occurred in part because the modern pseudoscience of race became a dominant explanation for differences between nations and other human groups. European colonial and imperial ambitions required a paradigm that could justify oppression of non-European peoples and theft of their land and resources. European concepts of race in the eighteenth and nineteenth centuries depended on the idea that members of a human 'race' share essential traits, both physical and non-physical, that they have collectively inherited from their ancestors.[59] In order to find roots that could be said to demonstrate their essential characteristics and superiority, European people and nations looked to both classical and medieval sources. Modern ideas about race, including whiteness, often build on medieval foundations.[60] This included (but was in no way limited to) reassessment and reimagining of Norse history and the Vikings in Scandinavian and other nations.

Paul-Henri Mallet, a Swiss-born intellectual, promoted medieval Norse myth, poetry, and culture in the 1750s, linking them directly to emerging modern versions of the older concept of a Gothic race (also variously termed Germanic or Teutonic), and laying foundations for ethnonationalist myth-making in Scandinavian countries

---

[58] We follow the general usage of referring to Norse people and cultures collectively, and Viking(s) specifically when Norse people travelled to engage in raiding or invasion.

[59] For accounts of whiteness and European ideas about race, see Heng, *Invention of Race*; Painter, *The History of White People*; Young, *The Idea of English Ethnicity*.

[60] Heng, *Invention of Race*. For the development of racial concepts and ideas in the Islamic world during this period, see Rachel Schine, 'Conceiving the Pre-modern Black Arab Hero', 301–4.

in the early nineteenth century.[61] In Scandinavian myth-making, 'the Viking past was owned solely by the Scandinavian nations' and the 'main themes' of Viking history 'were political unification, Viking voyages, and ... conversion to Christianity'.[62] Across Europe (and in Iceland), Norse cultures were taken 'to represent pre-classical barbarian culture', were part of 'the search for northern "primitive" ancestors,' and 'provide[d] indigenous European examples of Rousseau's "Noble Savage" that suited ethnonationalist Romantic impulses'.[63] Nations outside Scandinavia, however, also incorporated Norse culture and achievements into their own history and heritage and were able to do so because of Viking mobilities.

In England, for example, Mallet's ideas were adapted for an English audience by Thomas Percy in his *Northern Antiquities* (1770), which included a translation of some of Mallet's volumes.[64] Percy and his contemporaries, such as Richard Hurd and Thomas Warton, Gothicised English language, culture, people, and society in the 1760s and 1770s, retrofitting them and their ancestors into a larger Gothic white race which also included the Norse, Germans, and Normans.[65] Theories of the characteristics of this race, which were said to include a martial spirit and inherent love of freedom, were partially derived from the writings of the Roman author Tacitus, and were supposedly 'purer' in the racial stock of England and Scandinavia, owing to their remoteness from the rest of Europe.[66] This construction of a single Gothic race enabled all things Norse to be retrospectively claimed as the common heritage of England and its (former) settler colonies: '[O]n both sides of the Atlantic, the notion of an Anglo-Saxon race fortified by Viking blood gradually coalesced into an ideology that was reflected and refracted in the literary and historical writing of the nineteenth century.'[67] This spatial medievalism was variously practised in many Western European nations, including England, France, and Germany.

In Victorian Britain Vikings were figured in numerous ways that aligned with notions of ethnonational and imperial identity: as 'merchant adventurers, mercenary soldiers, pioneering colonists, pitiless raiders, self-sufficient farmers, cutting-edge naval technologists, primitive democrats, psychopathic berserkers,

---

[61] Clunies Ross and Lonnröth, 'The Norse Muse', 6–7. Richards, *Vikings*; Sundmark, 'Wayward Warriors', 198.

[62] Richards, *Vikings*, 119.   [63] Richards, *Vikings*, 117.

[64] Young, 'Thomas Percy's Racialization of the European Middle Ages'.

[65] Rix, 'Romancing Scandinavia'; Young, 'Thomas Percy's Racialization of the European Middle Ages'; Young, 'Race, Medievalism and the Eighteenth-Century Gothic Turn'.

[66] On the influence of Tacitus' writing on modern ideas, see Krebs, *A Most Dangerous Book*.

[67] Campbell, *Norse America*, 205. 'Anglo-Saxon' is a modern racial term linked to colonialism and imperialism; see Rambaran-Olm and Wade, 'The Many Myths of the Term "Anglo-Saxon"' and Rambaran-Olm, 'A Wrinkle in Medieval Time'.

ardent lovers and complicated poets'.[68] These sometimes conflicting figurations suited the ideological and political needs of a British empire expanding by an interlinked combination of military force and commercial power, dependent on 'ruling the waves' through its naval superiority, and invested in ideas of liberty and racial and cultural superiority to both inspire and justify its actions and ambitions. Norse ancestry and characteristics, as exemplified by Vikings, were constructed as underpinning the success of the British Empire.[69] These constructions appeared in high and popular culture as well as scholarship and politics.

In the USA accounts of Norse settlement in north America in the *Greenlanders Saga* and *Erik the Red's Saga* became widely known and were folded into ethnonationalist myth-making from the early nineteenth century. The 'Vinland voyages [have] provided a myth of national foundation by a Teutonic [read also Germanic or Gothic] hero who predated Columbus by some 500 years' since the nineteenth century in politics and popular culture alike.[70] Theories that Norse (and other European) peoples were substantially present in North America before Columbus undermine 'claims to Indian civilization and artisanship' through assertions that 'any and all sophisticated artifacts ... really belonged to the [supposedly] more advanced ancient arrivals'.[71] The short-lived Norse settlements in North America have taken on a far more significant role in the modern world as vectors for spatial medievalism than they ever had in Norse society in the Middle Ages. They are a powerful example in part because of the historical and archaeological record, but it is important to remember that the presence of Vikings on that continent is in no way related to white settlement there in later centuries. Spatial medievalism is also invoked in nations like Australia and New Zealand, where there is no medieval history of European settlement, in order to claim sovereignty and justify dispersal of Indigenous peoples.[72]

Nineteenth-century popular versions of Vikings and Norse people were reproduced in early twentieth-century films and through them into other 'popular reimaginings ... in comic strips, in animated and print cartoons, and in *bandes desinées* and graphic novels'.[73] This repetition reiterated spatial medievalisms in England and settler colonies. It was also taken up by Nazis in both Germany and Scandinavia. Nazi Germany 'wished to emphasize a unity with the people of Scandinavia which had little foundation in reality'.[74] A salient

---

[68] Wawn, *The Vikings and the Victorians*, 4.   [69] Wawn, *The Vikings and the Victorians*.

[70] Barnes, 'Nostalgia, Medievalism and the Vinland Voyages', 144. See also Barnes, *Viking America*.

[71] Kolodny, *In Search of First Contact*, 33.

[72] Davis, *Periodization and Sovereignty*; Young, 'A Decolonizing Medieval Studies?'.

[73] Harty, 'Introduction', 4.   [74] Richards, *Vikings*, 124.

illustration of their significance is that, in 1964, the US Congress proclaimed 9 October Leif Erikson Day, named after the leader of a saga expedition, but in truth commemorating the arrival of the ship *Restauration* from Norway to New York in 1825, traditionally seen as the start of immigration from Scandinavia to the United States. Every president since has issued a proclamation on that day invoking racial euphemisms and dog whistles to position the USA as a white nation with medievalist roots. Barack Obama's 2016 proclamation, for example, expresses 'appreciation for the myriad contributions of Nordic Americans' before reminding readers of 'the discovery that set this profound history in motion',[75] a clear assertion that the short-lived medieval Norse colonies in North America were the catalyst for both the United States in the present and its history of immigration.

Vikings in contemporary popular culture are invariably racialised as white and typically display 'Germanic' characteristics, as we discuss further later in this Element. Norse mythology is invoked around the globe by neo-Nazis and other white power groups, for example the white vigilant 'Sons of Odin', founded in Finland and now with chapters as far afield as Australia and Canada.[76] Viking settlements in North America are invoked by some white extremist groups[77] and are also common sites for alternate history novels; at least one self-identified American neo-Nazi has written an alternate history suggesting that Vikings colonised the Midwest.[78] The book repositions eighteenth- and nineteenth-century racist claims used to denigrate First Peoples and 'justify' their forced removal from their lands into the twenty-first-century popular sphere. The idea that some Norse people 'stayed behind' in Vinland – or other Norse colonies – is a staple of white assertions of racial continuity in North America which have been deployed in both mainstream and extremist attempts to challenge First Nations' sovereignty.[79] Whatever the specific political beliefs of their creators, such works narrativise fantasies of white presence and sovereignty in North America; popular culture not only reflects but reinscribes in new forms the storying of the white European Middle Ages over centuries.

Viking Encounters and Encountering Vikings

Tales of Viking mobilities have been part of medievalist popular culture in novels, films, television, games, and more since the nineteenth century. Popular

---

[75] 'Presidential Proclamation – Leif Erikson Day, 2016 | Whitehouse.Gov'.

[76] Castle and Parsons, 'Vigilante or Viking?'.   [77] Kaplan, 'The State of Vinland'.

[78] See Winthrop-Young, 'The Rise and Fall of Norse America'. We choose not to name the author or book to avoid providing potential readership.

[79] Richards, *Vikings*, 124–7.

culture representations of Vikings are dominated by white Western perspectives and ideologies even when they represent cross-cultural contact and mobility. Joseph Bruchac, a US author who has Abenaki heritage, wrote *The Ice Hearts* (1979), which, like *Skraelings*, tells of a First Peoples encounter with Vikings in North America, but with a limited print run of three hundred copies, it cannot be considered an example of 'popular' global medievalism. Michael Crichton's *Eaters of the Dead* (1976) and its film adaptation *The Thirteenth Warrior* (1999) are the most well known; they draw on the tenth-century writings of the Baghdad-based diplomat Ahmad ibn Fadlān and feature him as a central character. Both were written by white American men principally for Western anglophone audiences. *The Thirteenth Warrior* valorises white masculinities conventionally linked to Vikings[80] and reinforces medievalist stories of white superiority over other peoples.[81] The Syrian soap opera *Saqf al-Alam* (2007) reportedly recounts Ahmad ibn Fadlān's tenth-century journey from Baghdad to the court of the Volga Bulgars and was made in response to caricatures of the Prophet Mohammed that appeared in Danish newspapers in 2005. The series was available on YouTube for a period, but at the time of writing we have not been able to access it and therefore cannot include it further in our discussion here. The problem of accessibility, particularly for works that are not in English, is a significant challenge to counterstorytelling in popular culture. With the largest distribution channels, including Amazon, Netflix, and other streaming services, owned by and catering to mainly anglophone Western audiences, voices and perspectives from outside the West are rare.

Vikings *(2013–2020)*

Vikings (2013–20) was a Canadian History Channel programme with significant viewership around the world. At the time of writing, all six seasons are available through Netflix, giving it a substantial potential reach in the popular market beyond its original release. The show centres on the fictionalised lives of Ragnar Lothbrok and his family, covering an historical range of events from the sack of Lindisfarne in 793 CE to King Alfred's victory over a Viking army at the Battle of Edington in 878 CE. Parts of the narrative are inspired by Old Norse sagas and other sources that mention Ragnar or his sons, but their appearances during particular historical events of note are largely fictional. A salient example is when Ragnar's son Ubbe leads an expedition to North America in the final season, at least a century before Leif Erikson's historical journey. *Vikings* is part of the 'real' or 'gritty' medievalism that has dominated popular culture in the past decade or so, with a 'formulaic depiction of brutality, dirtiness, sex [and]

---

[80] Sklar, 'Call of the Wild'.   [81] Shutters, 'Viking through the Eyes of an Arab Ethnographer'.

violence' – albeit with less sex than other programmes in the subgenre – and typically reinforces white racial medievalist stereotypes.[82] *Vikings* is presented and has been generally received as historical fiction with an interest in authenticity, although Norse mythology and magic feature variously in it.[83]

Vikings endows significant mobility on its eponymous group and is representative of broader trends in representation of mobilities of and enabled by Norse people. The long run of the show enabled, or perhaps required, it to cover a substantial span of Viking mobility around the globe from Norway to England, Iceland, Sicily, Egypt, Greenland and North America, and the Silk Roads and Kiev. Conquest, raiding, colonisation, and trade variously inspire this breadth of travel in the interlaced storylines. The narratives also, however, frequently revolve around kingdom-building and unification in Norway, returning each season to conflicts over power, control, and the nature of Norse society, focussed at Kattegat. Kattegat and Norway more widely can thus be considered a 'mooring' for the mobilities that drive much of the narrative. The programme echoes, in these substantial storylines, nineteenth-century Scandinavian preoccupations with Viking history as outlined earlier in this Element. Norse conversion to Christianity is a significant theme, and in the first three seasons there is substantial movement of characters back and forth between England and Norway. England, like Norway, is a mooring in narratives of mobility. The series opens up its geographical reach in season four with narratives involving colonisation of Iceland, raiding and trading in Spain, Sicily and North Africa, and colonisation in North America interwoven with the ongoing narratives moored in England and Kattegat in the last three seasons.

Viking Centres

Viking mobilities between Scandinavia and England enabled the modern imagination of the racially pure but multinational Gothic identity outlined earlier in this Element, particularly in anglophone enthnonationalist circles. Thus mobility between England and Norway is a consistent feature of *Vikings* and is central to the storying of (eventually) a united white community in England. In the show's second episode, for instance, Ragnar returns to Kattegat with slaves and treasures from the sacked Lindisfarne monastery. He takes an English monk, Athelstan, as his slave and Athelstan eventually becomes part of his household. The Vikings raid Northumbria twice more in the first season. In the second season, four years later in the show's timeline,

---

[82] Elliott, "'Our Minds Are in the Gutter, but Some of Us Are Watching Starz ... '", 100. Young, *Race and Popular Fantasy Literature*, 63–85.

[83] For example, Chadwick, 'Fantasizing History'.

Ragnar lands in Wessex and expresses a desire to start a colony there. Finding himself in conflict with the local king, and with his own supposed allies back in Norway, he is forced to return there, leaving his army to be defeated and eventually absorbed into the kingdom of Wessex. This repeated movement between moorings, and the resulting settlement of Vikings in England in the first two seasons, establishes the pattern followed in subsequent seasons.

Over *Vikings'* six seasons, complex narratives drive movement between Norway and England. A multigenerational, interfaith conflict between pagan Vikings and Christian Saxons is resolved in a set of events that offers a framework for Vikings and other Norse people to become part of English society. In the series finale, Ivar the Boneless, one of Ragnar's sons and a symbol of the pagan gods, allows himself to be killed, prompting King Alfred, the Saxon leader, to command his armies to stop fighting. Alfred invites Hvitserk, another of Ragnar's sons, to live with him and his family, promising that they will 'discuss many important matters about our future together, and the future of our peoples'.[84] Hvitserk buries Ivar and renounces the Norse gods before being baptised as a Christian. Alfred stands as his godfather and names him 'a Christian Saxon prince'. Six seasons of interfaith conflict achieve closure by pointing towards a united future: the Gothicised England of nineteenth-century fantasies. The shift in representation of England from a source of wealth to be raided to a site for colonisation, putting down anchors, and interethnic alliances reiterates stories of transnational white racial connection and assimilation, as well as the claiming of Norse culture as heritage through spatial medievalism that now occurs throughout much of the Western world.

Travelling to and from the East

Once England and Norway are established as linked moorings in the first three seasons, *Vikings* opens up the scale and scope of its mobilities, including through travel to and from the East. Orientalism and medievalism, as John Ganim explores at length, have a 'twinned association' and both are paradigms of identity formation that are deeply concerned with origins.[85] If medievalism is crucial to white Western identity formations of self, Orientalism creates otherness. Orientalism is a set of stereotypical Western beliefs and assumptions about the people, cultures, and societies of the East that exoticises and denigrates them in ways that sometimes parallel temporal medievalism. According to these stereotypes outlined by Edward Said, the people of 'the east' (i.e. most of the Asian continent, sometimes overlapping with North Africa) are, among other things: 'gullible ... cunning ... liars' who are lazy, given to 'intrigue' and

---

[84] Hirst, *Vikings* 6.20.   [85] Ganim, *Medievalism and Orientalism*, 3.

cruelty, and 'in everything oppose the directness and nobility of the Anglo-Saxon race',[86] as well as overly and overtly sexualised.[87] Although, as pre-modern critical race scholars have demonstrated, versions of these stereotypes were in circulation during the medieval and early modern periods, Western popular culture has 'helped cement' in the present 'many of the ethnoracial stereotypes' that emerged in their modern forms in the eighteenth century.[88]

Orientalist stereotypes pervade the representation of mobilities in *Vikings*. The show follows Ragnar's sons as they variously raid and trade in Muslim Spain, Sicily, and North Africa, as well as along the Silk Roads in Eastern Europe, and all of these locations are presented through an Orientalist lens. Season six, for example, opens on 'The Silk Road'.[89] Images of dry, desert mountains, travel through snowy and dusty roads, and a market with exoticised Eastern people and goods (shaven-headed Buddhist monks, spices, camels, and the like) are intercut with shots of Ivar and Hvitserk staring around them. The sequence, which lasts for several minutes, emphasises the foreign strangeness of the people and places compared to the familiarity of Kattegat and England. Similar establishing sequences characterise the Mediterranean travels of Ivar's brother Bjorn in season four.

Bjorn's travel in the Mediterranean and Africa encodes substantial Orientalism. Christians and Muslims alike prove treacherous and barbaric. Having discovered that Euphemius, the Christian commander of Sicily, is also a client of the Muslim emir Ziyadat Allah, Bjorn and his companions ask to meet the latter in hopes of promoting trade. On the advice of a nun named Kassia, Euphemius agrees, but he is murdered by the emir's men during the meeting. Kassia proves to have been a seductive double agent and, to add a further layer of shock value, the emir's men cook and serve the murdered Euphemius to Bjorn and his companions, who only escape due to a conveniently timed sandstorm. Thus the East promises trade and riches but is revealed as a place of danger and deceit, exemplified in Kassia's beauty and treachery. The Vikings flee and do not return. Potential globality is reshaped into a story of Eastern otherness that closes off Viking mobility and redirects action to their moorings in north-western Europe.

Season four also introduces Yidu, one of several slaves from Asia captured during a raid in France and brought to Kattegat to be sold. Yidu gives painkilling drugs to Ragnar, who is suffering from wounds received in a raid, describing

---

[86] Said, *Orientalism*, 38–9.   [87] Said, *Orientalism*, 190.

[88] Hardy, 'Godless Savages and Lockstep Legions', 192. See the special issues of *New Literary History* 52 (2021) on race and periodisation and *Literature Compass* 18 (2022) on pre-modern critical race studies.

[89] Hirst, *Vikings* 6.1.

them as 'an ancient Chinese medicine'.[90] Ragnar becomes addicted to the drug, and is briefly lovers with Yidu, but in a later episode, after she threatens to reveal his secrets, he kills her. Although Yidu's presence draws attention to the globality of Europe in the Middle Ages, her character, like Kassia's, is constructed through Orientalist stereotypes which reinforce conventional white medievalism by othering her. Yidu is exoticised, feminine, and beautiful, as well as a treacherous purveyor of addictive drugs that threaten Ragnar's capacity to lead and fight. Her presence, particularly as Ragnar's lover, threatens narratives of Viking racial purity, but Ragnar's murder of her violently erases any possibility of a multiracial child and symbolically asserts white masculine rejection of Eastern femininity. This deadly expulsion of a character who embodies threatening Eastern otherness prevents any disruption of fantasies of white medieval racial purity.

Travelling West

Short-lived Viking settlements in North America, as discussed earlier in this Element, have underpinned Western spatial medievalisms for centuries. *Vikings* begins its account of mobility westward with the settlement of Iceland in season four, conceived as a direct response to the increasing centralised royal power and Christianisation of Norway, which aligns with nineteenth-century Scandinavian ethnonationalisms. In the first episode of season six, Ubbe Raganarsson says to his brother Bjorn, 'like our father I feel the compulsion, the need to go exploring again' and 'I was once told about a land, far to the west, a wanderer had glimpsed it from his boat. It's an uninhabited land, thickly forested, trees as high as mountains'.[91] The lines echo a passage in the *Greenlanders Saga*, inspired by Leif Erikson, about the sighting of a previously unknown land. Ubbe and his followers reach the American continent after a difficult voyage. They come upon a village of Mi'kmaq people and, after an initially tense moment that threatens violence, are welcomed.[92] When a Viking kills a Mi'kmaq man, Ubbe and the rest decide he must be executed 'or there will never be justice or trust in this new world'.[93] Ubbe says, 'we are to behave like different men and women, reborn in the image of this new land'. There is an element of exceptionalism here and this set of events positions the fictional Viking settlement in contrast with later white colonisation, forced dispossession, and genocide of Indigenous peoples.

White settler colonial possession nonetheless haunts the unfinished narrative of Ubbe's expedition. Looking out from a cliff over wooded valleys and

---

[90] Hirst, *Vikings* 4.4.   [91] Hirst, *Vikings* 6.01.   [92] Hirst, *Vikings* 6.19.
[93] Hirst, *Vikings* 6.20.

mountains in the final episode, Ubbe says: 'I see endless possibilities. I see a golden landscape. Rich farming soil, minerals, rivers, ports, construction, abundance . . . Everything that Ragnar [his father] dreamed of the first time he sailed away from Kattegat . . . this is what he was searching for.'[94]

The exchange makes clear that the multigenerational spirit of exploration that inspired Ubbe and his father and initiated substantial parts of the narrative of *Vikings* is in fact a spirit of colonisation. They do not wish to merely see the land or know what is there. They want to exploit its resources. Ubbe effectively prophesies white colonisation of the Americas in later centuries, inserting a decidedly modern vision for the land into the medieval past. This move retrospectively justifies spatial medievalism by positioning the failed Norse settlements in North America within the lineage of later white colonisation and ethnonationalisms. Ubbe, like Leif Erikson, embodies a particular facet of white identity formation that has been retrospectively imagined as shared among the white people of modern nations.

Decentred Vikings

Skraelings (2014) is a young adult historical novel that recounts Viking encounters with Indigenous peoples of what is now known as Baffin Island. The title is taken from the Old Norse word used in sagas for Indigenous peoples of North America, suggesting a Norse perspective, but this is not the case. *Skraelings* is a 'first-contact' novel that reverses the conventional perspective of popular culture narratives of Vikings in North America, and indeed of centuries of Western culture. The focalising character is a young Inuit hunter named Kannujaq. Vikings are peripheral in both the world and narrative of *Skraelings*, a positioning that sees the novel engage in counterstorytelling global medievalism. It deconstructs white colonial medievalism by inverting the colonial gaze and appropriates an element of Western culture to serve an Indigenous purpose; the book presents Inuit perspectives and ways of being.

There are two first-contact narratives in *Skraelings*, one between two Indigenous peoples – the Inuit and Tuniit – and another between those peoples and Vikings. Kannujaq has heard of both Tuniit and Vikings before, but has not encountered them himself. At the start of the novel he is out hunting with his dogs and becomes fearful when he sees piles of stones resembling people which are created by the Tuniit, 'a shy and bizarre folk who had occupied the Land long before the arrival of Kannujaq's family'.[95] The passage is one of several

---

[94] Hirst, *Vikings* 6.20.
[95] Qitsualik-Tinsley and Qitsualik-Tinsley, *Skraelings*, pt. 62. All citations are to the Kindle ebook edition and are therefore by part (location) rather than page number.

that emphasises the diversity of cultures and mindsets among the peoples of Baffin Island. The novel thus refuses monolithic colonial constructions of Indigenous peoples. Mobility and mooring are key differences between the peoples: Kannujaq, for example, cannot understand why the Tuniit will not leave their stone homes to avoid the Vikings and simply make camp somewhere inland as his family would have done, although he comes to accept it.

Kannujaq initially others both Tuniit and Vikings, but his preconceptions shift and the narrative gives the reader access to his feelings and thought processes as his attitudes and beliefs change. Tuniit, he soon learns, are not dangerous beasts as he had believed, but people like him: 'he was shocked to see how human they looked'.[96] Similarly, when he first sees Vikings he thinks they are not human, perceiving them as 'manlike certainly, but enormous in size, as though their mothers had become too friendly with bears'.[97] This introduction reverses the Western colonialist gaze that typically positions Indigenous peoples as less than human. As with the Tuniit, after a short time he realises that Vikings are in fact human, despite their differences to himself and his people.[98] In the space of a few hours, he greatly expands his view of humanity to encompass groups that are both new and different to him.

'First-contact' stories are a staple of historical fiction and 'the opening of an epoch and the joining of histories', but they also 'explain how things are now and ... contain a key to how they might be'.[99] In *Skraelings*, Kannujaq's first contacts with the Tuniit and Vikings come close together: he stumbles on a Tuniit village in the midst of a Viking raid. He initially expects the Tuniit to attack him, but they do not. Their child shaman, Siku, sees Kannujaq's presence as a sign and draws him into their conflict with the Vikings, whom he eventually helps them defeat. The violence of the Viking raid, however, shapes his first encounter with both peoples. Violence is alien to Kannujaq. It 'equalled madness' to his family but the Vikings bring it into his world.[100] He is changed by the violence of the Vikings, which prefigures the violence of later settler colonial nations in the Artic and other parts of the globe. 'The violence of others pulled him into a violent response ... peace is possible only if all possess the will for it. And Kannujaq, without even knowing that he was doing so, had shifted his role from hunter to warrior.'[101] This foreshadows the brutal future of

---

[96] Qitsualik-Tinsley and Qitsualik-Tinsley, *Skraelings*, pt. 109.
[97] Qitsualik-Tinsley and Qitsualik-Tinsley, *Skraelings*, pt. 85.
[98] Qitsualik-Tinsley and Qitsualik-Tinsley, *Skraelings*, pt. 213.
[99] Lutz, 'Myth Understandings', 1.
[100] Qitsualik-Tinsley and Qitsualik-Tinsley, *Skraelings*, pt. 169.
[101] Qitsualik-Tinsley and Qitsualik-Tinsley, *Skraelings*, pt. 757.

white European colonisation of North America in later centuries and its lasting violent legacies in the present.

Kannujaq eventually learns that the Viking leader, whom he dubs 'the Glaring One', was once shipwrecked and had lived with the Tuniit for some time before going back to his own people. He realises that the Glaring One is Siku's father and that the raids do not seek to recover iron swords, knives, and tools taken from the shipwreck by the Tuniit leader. Rather, 'as with Kannujaq's own folk, what mattered to the Glaring One was family'. It is Siku that they seek.[102] This recognition of a common value leads Kannujaq to wonder what the Glaring One's people are like: 'maybe they had more in common with Kannujaq's folk than he had wanted to admit, maybe they had just arrived in this area . . . maybe they had not done as well, in surviving the Land, as Kannujaq's people'.[103] This passage emphasises similarities between the Inuit and Vikings by drawing attention to their common mobility. Both have come to the Land from elsewhere, highlighting their similarity through contrast with the firmly anchored Tuniit. This common mobility negates the kind of racial exceptionalism often attached to Vikings in modern medievalisms (such as in Hillary Clinton's comments quoted at the beginning of this section), forecasts the failure of Norse settlements in North America, and emphasises the success of the Inuit in living in the Arctic. In doing so, it undercuts myths of white sovereignty developed from the medieval Viking presence in North America.

Skraelings actively rejects modern Western concepts of landownership and national territory: 'Humanity did not set limits of the Land. The Land set limits on humanity.'[104] The voice of the omniscient narrator addresses the reader directly at various points in the novel, including in a passage that explicitly defamiliarises modern concepts from Kannujaq's world: '[E]ven if, by some magic, you could have spoken a common language with him, your ideas of the world would have been very different . . . the easy part would have been explaining television and airplanes. But how would you have gotten across the idea of a country? Or a border?'[105]

These two passages taken together balance continuity and change: Kannujaq's understanding of his relationship with the land evokes contemporary Indigenous ways of being, but Inuit today also understand nations and borders in ways Kannujaq could not. By drawing attention to the socially constructed nature of nations and borders, *Skraelings* not only challenges specific white medievalist claims to sovereignty in North America, but defamiliarises Western concepts of sovereignty.

---

[102] Qitsualik-Tinsley and Qitsualik-Tinsley, *Skraelings*, pt. 842.
[103] Qitsualik-Tinsley and Qitsualik-Tinsley, *Skraelings*, pt. 847.
[104] Qitsualik-Tinsley and Qitsualik-Tinsley, *Skraelings*, pt. 39.
[105] Qitsualik-Tinsley and Qitsualik-Tinsley, *Skraelings*, pt. 34.

Vikings and Violence: Taking Possession

Comparison of *Skraelings* and the North American narrative in *Vikings* demonstrates that the former engages in critical counterstorytelling. In *Vikings*, the Mi'kmaq people chiefly function as a source of narrative tension in the Vikings' story; even the murder of one of them is principally an opportunity for development of Viking collective identity and Ubbe's leadership. In *Skraelings*, the Vikings, particularly their leader, serve the same purpose. Their raids are a plot device that brings Kannujaq into contact with other peoples and ways of being, resulting in personal growth for him and a new possibility for mutual understanding between the Tuniit and Inuit. Acknowledgement of the violent colonial future shapes the novel. Its focus on Kannujaq, and through him Inuit world views and ways of being, offers an alternate reality in which white colonisers recognised the humanity of Indigenous peoples and what they had in common. The global medievalism of *Skraelings* thus disrupts white medievalist stories about the past that position present power structure and oppression as natural and inevitable. In doing so, it invites readers to imagine a future that does not proceed from that white Western perspective but instead values the full humanity of all peoples and reimagines their relationship with the natural world.

Reading these texts together reveals that, if Vikings are an icon of medieval mobility, they are also an icon of violent white possession taking. As Aileen Moreton-Robinson argues, the territory of settler colonial states, such as the USA, Canada, and Australia, 'has been marked by and through violence and race'.[106] The violent characteristics of Vikings in twenty-first-century popular culture are rooted in the white racial imagination of the eighteenth century. Taking possession is the aim of Viking violence, and by extension Viking mobility, in both case studies: of slaves, riches, and land in *Vikings* and of Siku in *Skraelings*. In *Vikings*, the mutual shedding of blood by Saxons and Vikings enables creation of a Norse mooring in England and a bloody execution does the same in North America. In *Skraelings*, Viking violence unites the Tuniit and Inuit against them and violence is their legacy through the changes wrought in Kannajuq. White sovereignty, then, is the product of bloodshed. *Vikings*, like *Skraelings*, tells more than one 'first-contact' story: of the first raid on Lindisfarne, of Viking settlement in England, and of the Mi'kmaq people in what would eventually be called North America. All of the first-contact stories in both texts 'explain how things are' in the contemporary world still characterised by white racial possession and violence, but *Skraelings* offers 'a key to how they might be' different through its global medievalism.[107]

---

[106] Moreton-Robinson, *The White Possessive*, xiii.   [107] Lutz, 'Myth Understandings', 1.

Dealing with Dragons: Two Approaches to Global Medievalist Epic

We turn now from historical fiction to perhaps the best-known genre of popular medievalism – high fantasy. Some thirty years ago Norman Cantor praised C. S. Lewis and J. R. R. Tolkien as 'inventors of a medieval society we can believe in, project ourselves into, and enjoy'.[108] This is true up to a point; it is incumbent upon us to, as Mary Rambaran-Olm urges, 'interrogate who "we" and "our" refer to in written discourse and conversations' about the Middle Ages.[109] The popular fantasy genre conventionally repeats the vision of a bounded, white European Middle Ages that shaped the imagined worlds of Narnia and Middle-earth in the mid-twentieth century. The result is not merely racist, stereotypical representations of people and cultures, but othering built into the very structure of the narrative.

Fantasies – and speculative fictions more widely – are broadly understood as genres in which alternative ways of knowing, thinking, being, and doing can be presented, constructed, and explored. Fantastic texts are arguably more easily available to this kind of project than historical fictions precisely because they are widely understood by authors, fans, and scholars as tools for approaching reality through an impossible lens. Historical fiction, in contrast, is typically understood as showing a new dimension of the same reality through a lens ground into shape by the possible – that is, as needing to make meaning only within the bounds of the 'historically authentic'. As Ebony Elizabeth Thomas argues, 'when readers who are White, middle class, cisgender, heterosexual, and able-bodied enter the fantastic dream, they are empowered and offered a sense of transcendence', but those 'who have been endarkened and Othered by the dominant culture can never be plausible conquering heroes nor prizes to be won in the fantastic'.[110] She proposes that 'emancipation' from these structures and the limited and limiting positions they offer requires 'restorying', and she outlines six forms of doing so, focused on 'time, place, identity, mode, perspective and metanarrative', which we explore further in the next section.[111] Here we analyse two contemporary medievalist fantasy epics that expand the scope of imagined cultural geographies while retaining a significant mooring in Western medievalist 'Europe': George R. R. Martin's *A Song of Ice and Fire* (1996–) and Samantha Shannon's *The Priory of the Orange Tree* (2019).[112]

---

108 Cantor, *Inventing the Middle Ages*, 232–3.
109 Mary Rambaran-Olm, 'Sounds about White'.　　110 Thomas, *The Dark Fantastic*, 23.
111 Thomas, *The Dark Fantastic*, 156–64.
112 *Priory* is a recent example of a number of epic fantasy novels and series that resist masculinist, heterosexist, and Eurocentric genre tropes in settings constructed as 'authentic' or 'alternate' supernatural histories of Europe. An earlier example is Jacqueline Carey's nine-book Kushiel's Legacy series (2001–11), which is unfortunately outside the scope of this analysis, but its pedagogical potentiality is briefly discussed in Pask, 'Resistance to Teaching', 41–2.

Fantasy As Epic

Fantasy is the genre most willing to engage in epic narrative and world building in contemporary popular culture. Edward James, in his exploration of the fantasy trilogy as epic, offers Theodore Steinberg's account as a working definition: '[T]he epic is a narrative that focuses simultaneously on the lives of its characters and on a pivotal moment in the history of a community, whether that community be a nation or a people or the whole of humanity.'[113] Also relevant is Richard Martin's argument that 'epic is hugely ambitious, undertaking to articulate the most essential aspects of a culture', and that it is 'on the level of ideology a metonymy for culture itself'.[114] In order to create a believable 'Second World', the epic must function as a successful introduction to that world while telling a compelling story. Twenty-first-century epics can be identified across the media of popular culture, from novels to games, television, film, and multimedia franchises.[115]

Tolkien's *The Lord of the Rings* emerged from his own engagement with medieval literature and white Western medievalism more generally. He lamented 'the lack of unity in English mythology' in strikingly geographic terms, wishing for 'the tone and quality that I desired, somewhat cool and clear, be redolent of our "air" (the clime and soil of the North West, meaning Britain and the higher parts of Europe)'.[116] Thus, in creating the universe of Middle-earth, he was inspired by, building on and also competing with, the epic traditions of France (*The Song of Roland*) and Spain (*El Cid*); the status of both is underpinned by their own nineteenth-century nationalist and colonialist agendas.[117] Thus the genre of epic fantasy – in the West at least – has its roots firmly in Eurocentric medievalism, with all its attendant assumptions.[118] Not all contemporary epic is fantasy, and not all epic fantasy is medievalist, but the overlap between these categories is significant.

C. Palmer-Patel's account of 'the narrative structure of Heroic Epic Fantasy' provides some useful starting points. It is 'where the hero realises a messianic duty via a journey, one which results in a spiritual transcendence for the hero along with the salvation of the world by the act of healing or re-creating it, thereby fulfilling their destiny'.[119] The first epic under discussion is Martin's

---

[113] Steinberg, *Twentieth-Century Epic Novels*, 29. Quoted in James, 'Epics in Three Parts', 11.

[114] Martin, 'Epic As Genre', 18.   [115] Innes, *Epic*.

[116] Cecire, *Re-enchanted*, 56–7. She quotes Tolkien, *The Letters of J. R. R. Tolkien*, 144–5, letter 131.

[117] On France, see DiVanna, *Reconstructing the Middle Ages*; Warren, *Creole Medievalism*. On Spain and its former colonies, see Altschul, *Geographies of Philological Knowledge*.

[118] On the Eurocentrism of Middle-earth, see, for example, Balfe, 'Incredible Geographies?'; Young, *Race and Popular Fantasy Literature*, 15–39.

[119] Palmer-Patel, *The Shape of Fantasy*, 1.

unfinished *A Song of Ice and Fire* book series (1996–), adapted and provisionally completed as the eight-season TV series *Game of Thrones* (2011–19).[120] *A Song of Ice and Fire* takes place in a famously immersive universe – enough that medievalists spent much of the TV series' run correcting mistaken assumptions it fostered about the Middle Ages. We place it in conversation with Shannon's *The Priory of the Orange Tree*, which has been positioned in both trade reviews and fan discourse as a feminist, queer-friendly, and racially diverse alternative to *ASOIAF*.[121]

Cultural geography is interested in 'forms of difference, the material culture of groups, but also … the ideas that hold them together, that make them coherent'.[122] Applying it to immersive fantasy allows us to explore the relationship between the represented world of the text and the society and culture which produced it. We focus on journeys undertaken by central characters, and the cultural geography of the worlds through and in which they travel, to interrogate the power relations represented there. Do such mobilities mirror those of *Vikings*, as discussed in the previous section, to reinforce conventional Eurocentrism, or do they offer counterstories? Finally, we use Ulrich Beck's theorisation of a 'world-risk society' to examine the supernatural forces that threaten both nature and humanity in each narrative and how they are defeated.[123] Does countering a planetary threat at the pivotal point of imagined history require or create a global community? If we take the final seasons of *Game of Thrones* as indicative of where *ASOIAF* ultimately leads, Martin's narrative proves profoundly white and Western in its world view and priorities. *Priory*, published twenty years after the first *ASOIAF* novel, consciously resists those priorities and demonstrates a more global orientation, but, for a variety of reasons, it remains tied to Eurocentric assumptions.

The World of Ice and Fire

However one feels about *ASOIAF* or *Game of Thrones*, their influence cannot be denied, and central to that influence is the embrace of the same 'gritty' medievalism discussed in the previous section. Critics and fans alike have praised the depth and complexity of George R. R. Martin's world building, which has frequently been compared to Tolkien's. Martin has made self-deprecating remarks in interviews regarding his interest in aspects of narrative (e.g. Aragorn's tax policies) that Tolkien simply did not care about. But his series

---

[120] Hereafter *ASOIAF*.
[121] Trombetta, 'If You Love "Game of Thrones", Don't Miss the Feminist Epic "The Priory of the Orange Tree"'.
[122] Crang, *Cultural Geography*, 2.   [123] Beck, *World Risk Society*.

is still at its heart an epic fantasy, and the world building is therefore shaped around that structure.

Westeros is the narrative centre; violent struggle over its Iron Throne drives the plot and motivations of the major characters, even those with no interest in rule. Although it diverges in some ways from prior fantasy tropes, *ASOIAF* does reiterate the habitual whiteness of the genre. Helen Young has identified 'four interconnected elements of fantasy convention' from the 1980s and 1990s 'which contribute significantly to its habits of Whiteness: cultural and physical geography; medievalism; the somatic markers of protagonists; and race logics which connect physical and non-physical traits to biological descent'.[124] Although *Game of Thrones* did not start airing until 2011, the first book in the series, *A Game of Thrones*, was published in 1996 and fits firmly within Young's framework: 'full of violence, rape, mud, blood, and White people'.[125] Whether this trend will persist remains to be seen, as Martin has yet to announce a publication date for the long-awaited sixth novel, *The Winds of Winter*. We will therefore, to some extent, be relying on the final three seasons of *Game of Thrones* as indications of how Martin's narrative might play out.

Even the internal histories of Westeros, published during the long gap following the publication of *A Dance with Dragons* in 2011, are consciously medievalist, revealing 'a layered colonial structure that in many ways mirrors [that of] medieval England' as recounted in chronicles such as Geoffrey of Monmouth's *History of the Kings of Britain*.[126] This is especially evident in *The World of Ice and Fire*, a book Martin co-authored with 'superfans' Elio M. Garcia and Linda Antonsson, the style of which evokes chronicles and universal histories. It states that original inhabitants of Westeros were 'the children of the forest' who shared the land with 'a race of creatures known as the giants'.[127] The so-called First Men, who crossed from the then-adjoining continent of Essos, farmed and developed towns, pushing the indigenous inhabitants further north, their history echoing medieval European historiography as well as modern settler colonial and imperial discourses.[128] Following the First Men are the Andals, 'a race of tall, fair-haired warriors' who conquer the southern kingdoms but fail to take the northern half of the continent.

---

[124] Young, *Race and Popular Fantasy Literature*, 41.

[125] Young, *Race and Popular Fantasy Literature*, 79.

[126] Carroll, *Medievalism in* A Song of Ice and Fire *and* Game of Thrones, 110. See also Carroll, 'Barbarian Colonizers and Post-colonialism in Westeros and Britain'; Larrington, *Winter Is Coming*.

[127] Martin, García, and Antonsson, *The World of Ice and Fire*, 252.

[128] Carroll, *Medievalism in* A Song of Ice and Fire *and* Game of Thrones, 112–13. On England's medieval history of colonialisation and modern settler colonialism, see Young, 'A Decolonizing Medieval Studies?'

Their invasion and physical description parallel the Germanic invaders of Britain discussed in the prior section. Finally, Aegon the Conqueror, the first Targaryen king, is associated with William the Conqueror of England by his name and achievements. The creation of a 'medieval' and 'medievalist' history of repeated colonisation in the ancient past deepens the Eurocentrism – specifically, the Anglocentrism – of Westeros.

The World of Ice and Fire includes limited material about Essos and an account of each of the seven kingdoms of Westeros before turning to 'other lands beyond the seas'.[129] The text disclaims knowledge of far parts of Essos, Sothoryos, and Ulthos and other parts of 'the tapestry that we call the known world' because of their distance.[130] This brief accounts positions different places, people, and cultures as analogous to parts of Asia, Africa, and Australia and implies the Americas exist without giving an account of them. It constructs a world that might be global, or at the very least interconnected by trading and raiding networks. The island of Naath, for example, is 'northwest of Sothoryos in the Summer Sea', and loosely analogous to Sri Lanka. Its goods have historically been traded to Westeros, but slave raids have interfered so that its 'fine handicrafts, shimmering silks and delicate spiced wines . . . are seen less and less in the markets of the Seven Kingdoms'.[131] As D'Arcens argues, the volume 'refracts this fantastic-medieval world through the prism of modern geopolitics [to] portray Sothoryos like those modern nations that function as sites of labour and resources to be exploited by the wealthy and powerful Global North'.[132] 'Planetos', then, is in a global Middle Ages when the events of *ASOIAF* and *Game of Thrones* take place, but the storying done through those narratives does not represent this and is, rather, profoundly Eurocentric.

In terms of narrative structure, the majority of the narrators in the first five books are either explicitly or implicitly identified as white. The fourth and fifth books (*A Feast for Crows* and *A Dance with Dragons*) complicate this by introducing three point-of-view characters from the region of Dorne. Martin has indicated that Dorne was inspired by the Iberian Peninsula which, from the sixth century to the fifteenth, was partly or completely under Muslim rule, and he has stated that the most significant real-world analogue is the caliphate of Córdoba.[133] Dorne's history sets it apart from the rest of Westeros: it was independently settled by 'ten thousand ships' of Rhoynish refugees from

---

[129] Martin, García, and Antonsson, *The World of Ice and Fire*, 252.

[130] Martin, García, and Antonsson, *The World of Ice and Fire*, 282.

[131] Martin, García, and Antonsson, *The World of Ice and Fire*, 282.

[132] D'Arcens, *World Medievalism*, 2.

[133] Hardy, 'The Crack of Dorne'. The Dornish scenes in *Game of Thrones* were filmed in Granada and the actors playing the main Dornish characters were Latino (Pedro Pascal), North African (Alexander Siddig), and South Asian (Indira Varma).

'western Essos' between the Andal and Targaryen invasions,[134] resulting in the Dornish having 'queer customs'.[135] This prehistory constructs Dornish people as racially distinct from the rest of Westeros and more recently associated with the Orientalised continent of Essos. This mirrors eighteenth- and nineteenth-century racial medievalisms which positioned peoples and cultures of north-western Europe as 'pure' and peoples and cultures closer to the East and Africa as less pure because of resulting contact.[136] The Dornish, then, are white when they need to be, but are also Orientalised and other.

One of the 'queer customs' referenced in *The World of Ice and Fire* is direct rather than male primogeniture. Dorne's rulership has never been restricted by gender, unlike the rest of Westeros, which would rather go to war than be ruled by a woman. While these prior conflicts are mainly referenced in passing in *ASOIAF*, Martin has published two separate novellas and a 'history', *Fire & Blood* (2018), detailing these events in a similar chronicle style to *The World of Ice and Fire*.[137] Thus we can see not just Eurocentrism, but a particular strand of white Western misogyny underpinning the ruling structures of Westeros. It is that aspect of world building that *The Priory of the Orange Tree* subverts most successfully.

Paths of Virtu(dom)

Sara González Bernárdez rightly argues that epic fantasy is 'prominently euro- and male-centric' but that *The Priory of the Orange Tree* is 'female-coded not simply through its characters, but down to the very core of the world that it builds'.[138] The novel also works to 'code' the core of its world in ways that challenge convention – Shannon has described *Priory* as a feminist retelling of St George and the dragon.[139] Divisions of cultural geography structure the novel and its imagined world; each chapter is titled with a compass point, most often 'East', 'West', and less frequently 'South', depending on where the action takes place. The entire world is pre-industrial, although gunpowder and guns appear. There are four narrative perspectives – two women from the East (Tané) and South (Ead) and two men, both from the West (Loth and Niclays), all of whom undertake significant journeys across geographic and symbolic borders. The geographical, social, and cultural divisions within the

---

[134] Martin, García, and Antonsson, *The World of Ice and Fire*, 21.

[135] Martin, García, and Antonsson, *The World of Ice and Fire*, 241.

[136] See our discussion of Vikings in the previous section.

[137] HBO's series *House of the Dragon*, focussed on the Targaryen civil war, and the brief reign of Queen Rhaenyra, started airing in August 2022 when this book was already in press, so it is outside the scope of our present discussion.

[138] Bernárdez, 'The Heroine's Journey', 93.   [139] Shannon, 'Damsels Undistressed'.

world are variously bridged throughout the novel; making connections is a central theme. Their journeys all have specific motivations and aims but ultimately serve to defeat the planetary-scale threat of the Nameless One; a flame-breathing draconic foe of legend trapped beneath the ocean at the start of the novel.

The 'West' is synonymous with 'Virtudom' and defined by a chivalric code of Six Virtues established by 'Saint Galian Berethnet', who supposedly defeated the Nameless One a thousand years before and whose descendants still rule Inys, an island in the north-west corner of the map clearly meant to evoke Britain. The societies of Virtudom are conventionally chivalric and feudal, ruled by royal families, with a social hierarchy of nobility and peasantry. Queen Sabran of Inys is also the spiritual leader of Virtudom as a whole (another echo of Britain, if more early modern than medieval). Hroth, which has a colder climate and borders arctic frozen lands, is across the sea to the north. Yscalin, once part of Virtudom but recently fallen to draconic worship, is across the sea to the south. Mentendon, across the sea to the south-east of Inys, is the only Western country to trade with the East. Niclays, an alchemist from Mentendon, has been banished there by Queen Sabran at the start of the novel. Three deliberate decisions from Shannon separate the West from conventional fantasy medievalist Europe: its religion is headed by a women and rule of Inys is matrilineal; same-sex relationships are permitted, if not fully sanctioned; and its people are not all phenotypically white. Loth, for example, has 'deep black skin'[140] while Niclays has yellow hair 'like straw'.[141]

The 'South' refers to the kingdom of Lasia, whose foundational belief sits in direct opposition to that of Virtudom: that a woman of the South, Cleolind Onjeyu, defeated the Nameless One a thousand years earlier, rather than Galian Berethnet. While not at war, Inys and Lasia have a historically fractious relationship and there is little contact between them outside of formal diplomacy. These two foundational myths come into direct conflict in the narrative of Ead Duryan, who was born and raised in the South but opens the novel serving as lady-in-waiting to Queen Sabran of Inys. She is described as having 'smooth and golden-brown' skin with hair that 'curled like wood shavings' and is 'thick and dark'.[142] In this description she is a spectacle for Tané, who is from the East, not for Westerners, but she is assumed to look typical for the South.

The East is separated from the other regions by religion, society, culture, and a vast ocean. It is constructed as analogous to East Asia, with the two realms of Seiiki and the Empire of the Twelve Lakes representing Japan and China, respectively. Both are closed to the West with the sole exception of an island

---

[140] Shannon, *Priory*, 14.　　[141] Shannon, *Priory*, 4.　　[142] Shannon, *Priory*, 723.

enclave in Seiiki that trades with Mentendon, and both are constructed through stereotypes. They have rigid honour systems, brutal laws are enforced by local officials without jury trial, and large bureaucracies wield significant power. Even without the physical barrier of the ocean, the East and the West are deeply divided in their attitudes to and experience of dragons. The kingdoms of the East revere dragons as powerful creatures of water and foes of the Nameless One, while the kingdoms of the West fear them as fire-breathing servants of the Nameless One. The division of humanity into 'wyrm killers' and 'wyrm lovers' thus has roots in real experience but is also a source of mutual fear and enmity not least because those differences in the nature of dragons are not respectively known. The great challenge in the novel lies in bringing together all these fragmented factions to prevent the Nameless One from returning and bringing about the end of their world.

Shannon's world building can be read as counterstorytelling that subverts many of the Eurocentric conventions that Martin's narrative upholds. Not everyone in Inys is white, and the presence of people of colour is unremarkable, as is the presence of women in positions of power, and, to a lesser extent, same-sex relationships. However, Orientalist stereotypes are left largely unexamined. The South exists principally as an indistinct otherland in the cultural geography of the world, meant to be the opposite of Virtudom and the repository of historical truth, but without internal motivation or a distinct culture outside the eponymous Priory of the Orange Tree. The East, meanwhile, is 'fantasy Asia' without critique or deconstruction of the Western perspectives and stereotypes encoded in the way it is constructed. More nuanced treatments of Central, South, and East Asian medievalisms are discussed in the subsequent section.

At the end of the novel, Sabran tells Ead she plans to initiate a 'Great Reformation' which includes her own abdication and a gesture towards democracy as a means to 'shake the very foundations of successions' (see Figure 1).[143] Her motivation is that 'a woman is more than a womb to be seeded', but the mention of 'Reformation' links this plan directly to the Protestant Reformation, which is often, rightly or wrongly, used to mark the end of the medieval and beginning of the modern. There is no suggestion that any such social and cultural shift will take place in Seiiki or the Empire of the Twelve Lakes excepting a brief remark by the Emperor that an alliance against the Nameless One and potential trade with the West is 'step towards modernity'.[144] *Priory* thus renders the East unable to progress except through contact with the West, even as it works to deconstruct fantasy conventions of white medievalism in other ways. This suggests that centring 'Europe' in the cultural geographies of fantasy worlds at the

---

[143] Shannon, *Priory*, 798. [144] Shannon, *Priory*, 688.

Figure 1 Ead and Sabran, for Pride Month 2021. Digital illustration by Salome Totladze, copyright 2021. Image appears with kind permission of the artist.

very least limits their potential for global medievalism to its deconstructive elements. What, then, of the journeys that cross physical and cultural borders in epic fantasy worlds?

Essos and the Wester(osi) Gaze

For the numerous Westerosi exiles in *ASOIAF*, Essos is constructed as a place of potential refuge, a wretched hive of scum and villainy, and a source of potential power open to exploitation to enable their return. That they wish to return is, at least up to this point in the books, a prevailing assumption. While much could be said of mobilities within Westeros, for purposes of this Element, it is more productive to interrogate those journeys that take place outside its borders. Essos, like Dorne, is principally constructed through Orientalist stereotypes in both *ASOIAF* and *Game of Thrones* – that is, as 'barbarian other' to the (relatively) civilised white Western self of Westeros.[145] This manifests in almost every aspect of how the place and people are constructed in the franchise, from racialised gender,[146] to stereotypical representation of peoples, places, and cultures.[147] This Orientalism positions Essos as open to exploitation of resources by Westerosi people. Both Arya Stark and Daenerys Targaryen 'pick and choose' from its people and cultures, and both take a 'colonial' approach in 'an extraction of Eastern labour and resources' for their own purposes.[148]

Arya has, thus far in the novels, spent little time in Essos, and the bulk of both scholarly and fan discussions of her arc tend to focus on her refusal to conform to gender expectations. However, as Hardy argues, her training with the Faceless Men of Braavos is constructed through a 'trope of military Orientalism: the ninja assassin'.[149] After her circuitous and traumatic journeys around war-torn Westeros, Arya travels to Braavos to learn to be an assassin, presumably in order to kill the enemies whose names she lists every night before she goes to sleep. This is in spite of her mentor's warning that, if this is her goal, she has 'come to the wrong place. It is not for you to say who shall live and who shall die'.[150] Arya chooses to retain her identity in deliberate contravention of the rules and values of the Faceless Men. Indeed, as Carole Jamison observes, her training 'eventually strengthens, rather than erases, Arya's identity' as it was supposed to.[151] In season six of *Game of Thrones*, she reasserts her identity as Arya Stark and returns to Westeros to wreak bloody vengeance through her newly acquired ability to 'say who shall live and who shall die'.[152]

Daenerys' long journey through Essos has been characterised as both a 'white saviour' narrative[153] and specifically US imperialist discourse.[154] She is introduced as a teenaged refugee from Westeros, marked out from the people around her by her silver hair and violet eyes, both of which connect her to a fallen empire of dragon lords.[155] She is also homeless, penniless, and under the control of her

---

[145] Carroll, *Medievalism in* A Song of Ice and Fire *and* Game of Thrones; Hardy, 'Games of Tropes: The Orientalist Tradition in the Works of G. R. R. Martin'.

[146] Downes and Young, 'The Maiden Fair'.   [147] Hardy, 'The East Is Least'.

[148] Hardy, 'Godless Savages and Lockstep Legions', 207.

[149] Hardy, 'Godless Savages and Lockstep Legions', 205.

[150] Martin, *A Feast for Crows*, 351.   [151] Jamison, 'A Girl Is Arya', 165.

[152] At the end of *A Dance with Dragons* she is still in Braavos, but an excerpt from the forthcoming *The Winds of Winter* reveals she retains her identity as Arya; she recognises and kills a Westerosi guard who had murdered one of her friends in an earlier book.

[153] Carroll, *Medievalism in* A Song of Ice and Fire *and* Game of Thrones, 127–30.

[154] Hartnett, '"The Silver Queen."'

[155] Martin once responded to a BIPOC fan on his blog that he briefly considered making the Targaryens dark-skinned, with the same silver hair and violet eyes, but that 'that choice would have brought its own perils'. Martin, 'We're Number One … " *House of the Dragon*, which depicts an earlier Targaryen civil war, features characters of Valyrian heritage played by Black actors. Martin's descriptions in *The World of Ice and Fire* and *Fire & Blood* implied that they

vicious elder brother, who intends marry her to a warlord in exchange for
a promised army with which to reclaim the Iron Throne. After his death she
takes up this goal, though she has no memory of Westeros and has spent her entire
life in Essos. Her subsequent journey is one of imperial acquisition enabled not just
by her possession of three fire-breathing dragons, but also by her race: 'she uses her
whiteness to gain power, amass an army, and conquer'.[156] The narrative supports
this by presenting her conquests through Orientalist caricature, a largely undiffer-
entiated series of awful men upon whom she is clearly a vast improvement.
Furthermore, her own history of sexual assault and slavery make her potentially
sympathetic as she and her supporters cast her as the 'breaker of chains', a one-
woman crusader against the slave trade. Martin has likened her failed attempt to
rule over one of her conquered cities to the US occupation of Iraq, which began
while he was writing the fourth and fifth books. This point was echoed by fellow
fantasy author Saladin Ahmed in his critique of *Game of Thrones*, where he
remarked that the 'troubling racial assumptions and caricatures' in Daenerys'
storyline were just 'a powerful reflection of America's' own race problems.[157]

Where one can find glimmers of a global medievalist world in Martin's
universe is within the fandom, where transformative fanworks often highlight
elements within their source text that are lacking or unexplored. Figure 2 draws
on medieval Central and West Asian cultural signifiers to capture a moment
briefly glanced at in the books of companionship between Daenerys and the
Dothraki women surrounding her. In the books, Daenerys has yet to leave the
East, but *Game of Thrones* saw her abandon her colonial project and, having
gained an army, resume her quest for the Iron Throne. Thus all roads, however
circuitous and exoticised, still ultimately lead to Westeros.

Global Journeys in *The Priory of the Orange Tree*

The main characters in *The Priory of the Orange Tree* undertake a variety of
challenging journeys before being drawn to the final confrontation with the
Nameless One at the Abyss. The connections between these mobilities and
character arcs are explored elsewhere, so we restrict our discussion here – as
with *ASOIAF* – to the spectrum of mobilities on display, the interactions between
characters and their locations, and the power relations implied therein.[158]

Three anchors draw together the variously mobile characters and their narratives: Ascalon, capital of Inys and centre of Virtudom in the West; the Priory of
the Orange Tree in the South; and the Abyss, which marks the divide between

---

were originally envisioned as white, leading to racist backlash from some fans. Martin himself
has approved the casting choices.
[156] Hartnett, "'The Silver Queen,'" 155.   [157] Ahmed, 'Is "Game of Thrones" Too White?'.
[158] Bernárdez, 'The Heroine's Journey'.

Figure 2 Daenerys and her companions. Digital illustration
by Şebnem Düzen, copyright 2019. Image appears with kind permission
of the artist.

East and West, where the Nameless One has been entombed. The spread of the
cultural geographies in which these anchors are located reflects and reinforces the
globality of the medievalist world. All of the major journeys in *Priory* take
characters into danger, sometimes from physical phenomena – the heat and
drought of the desert or storms on the open sea – or for reasons rooted in either
cultural difference or the supernatural. Tané's mobilities, like Arya's and
Daenerys', are at least initially driven by forces beyond her control, as when her
dragon is kidnapped by pirates. Ead's, on the other hand, are rooted in her often
contradictory missions and loyalties. She travels across Inys in search of information and magical artefacts to use against the Nameless One. Loth and Niclays are
both exiled from Inys against their will – Niclays to the trading enclave on Seiiki
and Loth as an unofficial ambassador to Yscalin, essentially a death sentence since
that kingdom fell under draconic control. He makes a harrowing escape into Lasia,
where he is confronted with information that shakes his world view, which he then
is compelled to deliver to the queen of Inys in person. His second journey, as an
ambassador, takes him first to the East, then, in the company of the emperor and his
forces, to the Abyss to battle the Nameless One.

Tané, Ead, and Niclays are also present at that final confrontation, arriving via circuitous routes across the borders of their respective worlds. The high level of mobility among the protagonists enables each to learn important new information previously unknown in their own territories (if at all), and, crucially, to share it with others. Perhaps the most prominent example is the existence of multiple types of dragons – knowledge that proves vital to the protagonists' efforts to avert the rise of the Nameless One and that prompts the West to seek an alliance with the East. The alliance is not merely a temporary one to defeat a mutual enemy, but looks to a future beyond that where the Abyss has been 'bridged' and 'trade' and 'shared knowledge' make the world more global.[159] Each character learns something that contributes, either directly or indirectly, to their collective defeat of the Nameless One.

Wyrms and White Walkers: World Risk

If epic is about a hero and their immediate community, then the pivot point in their trajectory is almost without exception one with much larger implications, such as large-scale or even planetary risk. The Others in *ASOIAF* and the Nameless One in *Priory* threaten destruction of not only the communities represented by individual heroes, but the entire world which exists beyond them. Ulrich Beck's theorisation of 'world-risk society' was developed in reference to modern globalisation in which all parts of the world are connected by a single vast network, rather than the globality of the Middle Ages in which multiple networks intersected.[160] It is nonetheless a useful concept for understanding how planetary threats are constructed and defeated. Beck argues that a 'world risk' such as climate change is of scale and nature that must be addressed cooperatively rather than by individual nations acting unilaterally. For Beck, this necessitates a reorientation of the historical drivers of action: '[T]he past loses its power to determine the present. Instead, the future – something non-existent, constructed or fictitious – takes its place as the cause of present experience and action.'[161] A 'world-risk society', then, necessitates counterstorytelling to deconstruct and negate the power of established ideologies, discourses, and conventions, and aligns with a global rather than insular European Middle Ages. In fantasy, an alliance typically manifests as historically and habitually hostile groups overcoming past differences to fight against world risks, but, as seen in Tolkien's alliance between Men, Elves, and Dwarves against the forces of Mordor, these are typically Eurocentric and short-lived. Responses to world risks in epic fantasy do not conventionally lead to formation

---

[159] Shannon, *Priory*, 687.   [160] Beck, *World Risk Society*, 23.
[161] Beck, *World Risk Society*, 137.

of a 'world-risk society'; the medievalist worlds they imagine typically are not and do not become global.

The specific nature and origins of the world-risk force in fantasy are significant. Martin's Others (called White Walkers in *Game of Thrones*) are powerful supernatural creatures from beyond the Wall that marks the limit of human civilisation in Westeros.[162] They have scarcely appeared in the extant novels, and the only thing known for certain about them is that their touch can raise and control the dead. Martin has specified in interviews that the Others in the books were partly inspired by stories of the fae from Celtic mythology, as well as classic horror films such as Romero's *Dawn of the Dead* and, more implicitly, the looming threat of climate change. In the HBO series, although they are not explicitly constructed through racist stereotypes, their vast numbers align them with conventional racialised enemies of 'good' in medievalist fantasy, and the threat they pose to the Wall resonates profoundly with contemporary discourses and anxieties about the integrity of borders and 'waves' of immigration.[163] The emergence of this threat reinforces the Eurocentricity at the heart of the franchise by making Westeros and its people the focus of the world-risk narrative. While there are brief references in *The World of Ice and Fire* to similar global threats in other parts of the universe, these are usually accompanied by dismissive commentary from the faux-historian narrator as a tongue-in-cheek nod to the reader, who is already aware from the main series that the Others are a real threat. Even the early account of their invasion from beyond the Wall is discredited as an attempt by 'the Night's Watch and the Starks to give themselves a more heroic identity as the saviours of mankind', another moment of brief fourth-wall breakage given that the Starks are the heroes of the series.[164] Notwithstanding Martin's playful approach to historiography, the Eurocentricity of his universe, where only white 'heroes are constructed as saviours', goes unexamined.[165]

In season eight of *Game of Thrones*, the community that gathers at Winterfell to stand against the oncoming army of the dead includes forces from Westeros and Essos. The Starks lead the majority of the people from Westeros proper, but they are joined by the remainder of the Night's Watch and the Wildlings from beyond the Wall, as well as Daenerys' invading force of Essosi and dragons. It is Arya Stark, however, who stabs the Night King with a dagger of dragonglass, and his death destroys the entire army in an instant. The eucatastrophic moment

---

[162] For ease of reference, and to distinguish between the unfinished books and the concluded TV series, we refer to them here as White Walkers.

[163] See, for example, Huysmans, *The Politics of Insecurity*.

[164] Martin, García, and Antonsson, *The World of Ice and Fire*, 12.

[165] Balfe, 'Incredible Geographies?', 79.

positions Arya as the sole hero, making the struggles, deaths, and even presence
of the alliance of otherwise warring parties irrelevant. The conflict in *Game of
Thrones* does not end with the defeat of the Night King, but with the ascension
of a new ruler to the Iron Throne. It is, therefore, a white national rather than
a global epic in the end.

In *Priory of the Orange Tree*, the Nameless One and his minions threaten
both the West and East and it is eventually determined that 'the last stand of
humanity will take place betwixt and between the two sides of the world' near
the Abyss.[166] This decentring of the world risk reflects the globality that
structures *Priory*. It requires, moreover, a purposeful and conscious rejection
of past enmities to focus instead on actions in the narrative present that can
result in a desired collective future that aligns closely with Beck's formulation
of the world-risk society. The alliance formed requires all involved to 'set aside
centuries of fear and suspicion',[167] and is for 'this day and for the rest of time' –
that is, future-oriented beyond defeat of the immediate threat.[168] Rulers of
realms in the West and East lead their armadas to the Abyss to fight the
Nameless One; everyone must leave the borders of their own power and trust
in their counterparts to do so. On a more individual level, Ead and Tané must
overcome ingrained distrust of each other as 'wyrm-killer' and 'wyrm-lover'[169]
to work together to trap the Nameless One beneath the ocean, this time
permanently: '[T]hey played this final game by turns, never breaking their
hold on each other. They spun him a cocoon, two seamsters weaving with the
waves.'[170] It is symbolically significant to the deconstruction of medievalist
fantasy convention and the white masculinist Western ideologies that underpin
it that two women of colour *not* from the West, and one of them queer, rather
than a white heterosexual man, kills the source of world risk. While Arya Stark
is a woman, she is a white heterosexual woman whose success upholds a white
patriarchal system, and her single-handed, climactic dispatch of the Night King
does not, in the end, bring about peace.

Counterstoryingtelling and Conventions

The medievalism and Orientalism conventional to Western popular epic fantasy
demonstrate that these texts are 'socially embedded, and draw upon pre-existing
cultural discourses', including but not limited to racial medievalisms.[171] The
narrative self of Martin's franchise is unquestionably white, but this is not the
case in *Priory* where the four focalising characters are from different cultural

---

[166] Shannon, *Priory*, 721.   [167] Shannon, *Priory*, 686.   [168] Shannon, *Priory*, 758.
[169] Shannon, *Priory*, 624.   [170] Shannon, *Priory*, 782.
[171] Balfe, 'Incredible Geographies?', 76.

geographies and where only one (Niclays) is phenotypically white; Loth, also from the West, is black. This disrupts genre conventional and broader cultural associations between whiteness and medieval Western Europe; no one is surprised that a man with black skin is a nobleman from Inys or that Sabran's retinue comprises people of different phenotypical races. *Priory* thus subverts the conventional cultural geographies evident in *ASOIAF* and its franchise, working in a deconstructive globalising medievalist mode. However, both texts reproduce Orientalist discourse in their construction of the East/Essos as largely unknowable to characters from the medievalist West/Westeros. The temporal medievalism in *Priory* that positions the East as only capable of approaching modernity through contact with the West echoes the positioning of Essos in *ASOIAF* as barbaric and backward, most notoriously through its reliance on the slave trade, which has been banned in Westeros. While the East in *Priory* is largely presented through a neutral lens, many of its intricacies remain unexplained and unexplored.

Mobility is central to both our case studies, but there are significant differences between them that reflect their relative repetition and subversion of genre convention and associated discourses. In the *Game of Thrones* franchise, two anchors draw together the multiple characters and their narratives: Winterfell and King's Landing. Both are within Westeros with positioning that emphasises the Eurocentricity of the franchise and its failure to imagine a global fantasy Middle Ages. *Priory* gestures towards a more diverse imagined world, but its limitations suggest that other approaches that decentre Europe altogether might be more fruitful, as is discussed in the subsequent section.

A World Elsewhere: Reimagining Global Medievalisms in Fantasy

It would not be an exaggeration to say that fantasy readers today are fortunate to have the beginnings of a genuinely diverse genre – and that it took a lot of work to reach that point. Plenty of ink has been spilled, by the authors of this Element, among others, on the (often unbearable) whiteness of medievalist fantasy from J. R. R. Tolkien and C. S. Lewis to J. K. Rowling and George R. R. Martin and beyond, as the previous section explored. Overwhelmingly, contemporary Western fantasy literature still takes place in what Maria Cecire describes as 'imaginary realms of magical medievalisms where white English power is still in its youth, on the rise, and bursting with globe-conquering potential'.[172] White Western medievalism, moreover, contributes substantially to the racisms and other marginalisations that structure fantastic narratives. *The Priory of the Orange Tree*, with its deconstruction of white Western epic fantasy convention

---

[172] Cecire, *Re-enchanted*, 187.

and centring of female heroes of colour, is arguably an example of counter-storytelling through restorying of place and identity, but, as discussed in the previous section, there are still limitations to these approaches.

One of our goals in this Element, as we noted in the introduction, is to highlight counterstories to those tired tropes – medievalist works that genuinely and consciously decentre white European perspectives or that transform and reinterpret the existing Eurocentric canon to make it as nuanced and complex as the societies that produced it. We focus here, then, on a selection of fantasy works, particularly by authors who identify as BIPOC, with an eye to the multiplicity of possible stories. The section draws on Thomas' 'restorying' framework to help position those works within the wider genre context of fantasy and to identify forms that have potential to do decolonising, global medievalist work outside it. We begin with an exploration of epic fantasy that decentres Europe altogether, as opposed to deconstructively engaging with existing white Western medievalisms: Chakraborty's Daevabad Trilogy (2018–20). We then turn to contemporary Arthuriana with an exploration of recent trends to restory, re-envision, and transform what we term the Arthurian Extended Universe in the twenty-first century. The works discussed in this section reflect what Cecire calls 'the increased visibility of fiction and fan communities that reflect an array of ethnic and cultural traditions, and which centre underrepresented character perspectives and relationships', and thus contribute to the counterstorytelling process of global medievalism.[173]

Recentring the Medievalist Fantasy World: The *Daevabad Trilogy*

The City of Brass (2017), the first book in Chakraborty's Daevabad Trilogy, opens in eighteenth-century Cairo, a city trapped between the Ottoman and nascent French empires, but does not stay there long. This choice on the author's part, to start her fantasy novel at the beginning 'of Western colonialism of the Middle East', positions the first of her protagonists as modern(ish) before entering what proves to be a medievalist fantasy universe.[174] The brief reference to the French invasion of Egypt positions the novels within human history, but also specifically places Europe at the periphery of the narrative. Unlike Tolkien's Middle-earth, Martin's Westeros and Essos, and the universe of *The Priory of the Orange Tree*, that of the Daevabad Trilogy maps directly onto our own. The map at the opening of each novel overlays central Asia, the Middle East, India, and East Africa, and is labelled with the names of the various djinn realms; the eastern edges of Europe are on its fringes but are so peripheral they are never named. This geography reflects the trilogy's roots in the rich and

---

[173] Cecire, *Re-enchanted*, 221.   [174] James, 'S A. Chakraborty'.

geographically widespread cultural traditions surrounding djinn, as well as the expansive and complex history of Islam and the Islamic world.

'Historical fanfiction' is the term Chakraborty herself uses to describe her imagined world, all but inaccessible to humans, where djinn exist uneasily alongside other powerful creatures from Middle Eastern mythology. Nahri, a young con artist from our world, accidentally summons a djinn during one of her fraudulent ceremonies and is pulled into a centuries-old supernatural conflict in an alternate version of Central Asia populated by six tribes of djinn. The six tribes, the reader discovers, were scattered thousands of years earlier by the powerful magic of the Prophet Suleiman (aka King Solomon), who 'stripped [them] of [their] abilities with a single word and commanded that all the daevas come before him to be judged'.[175] As Chakraborty explains:

> In Islam, you have humans, angels, and all these other creatures, including the djinn, who are created from smoke or fire. They live alongside us, but you can't see them, and they live for hundreds and thousands of years. As a history lover, I thought that was just great ... I tried to imagine how their civilization might have been built alongside ours.[176]

The use of djinn lore and the evocation of specific elements from Middle Eastern and North and East African history allow Chakraborty to create an immersive world that contains not one single white European yet feels unmistakeably *medieval* in its own way. While the negative connotations of the word in relation to Islam and Muslims must be acknowledged, the sense in which we use it here points to the functionally pre-modern society and culture of the world of the djinn and the city of Daevabad in particular, where magic largely keeps industrialisation at bay. The last major conflict in Daevabad's history when Nahri first arrives is the conquest of the city by djinn from Am Gezira (the Arabian Peninsula), roughly coinciding with the sixth-century military campaigns of the Prophet Muhammad and his immediate successors in our world. This decentring of Europe, its people and cultures, resonates with the orientation of the global Middle Ages and of global medievalism as we have theorised it in this Element.

The trilogy's two other protagonists are both, in different senses, 'from' Daevabad and therefore part of the medievalist universe. Darayavanoush (called Dara) is the supernatural entity accidentally summoned by Nahri in Cairo. Dara determines that she is part djinn (the offspring of humans and djinn are known as *shafit*) and that she is a long-lost member of the former ruling

---

[175] Chakraborty, *The City of Brass*, 106–7.

[176] James, 'S A. Chakraborty'. For an overview of djinn lore and mythology, see El-Zein, *Islam, Arabs, and the Intelligent World of the Djinn*. For an accessible introduction to Middle Eastern history, see Olomi, *Head on History*.

family of Daevabad, the Nahids. Dara is wrestling with his own bloody history of slavery and oppression, as well as his loyalty to Nahri's ancestors and his hatred for the current rulers of Daevabad, including the book's third protagonist, Alizayd Al Qahtani. Ali is the younger son of Daevabad's ruler and is himself of mixed djinn heritage – his father, Ghassan, is from the highly militaristic Am Gezira and his mother is from the wealthy and cosmopolitan kingdom of Ta Ntry (Somalia/Swahili coast). Unlike Nahri, whose religious scepticism fits her role as reader-avatar, Ali is a devout Muslim, while Dara follows the much older religion of the *daevas*, derived from Zoroastrianism.[177]

The magical city of Daevabad, created in the middle of an enormous lake, is the primary setting for the first two books of the series, *The City of Brass* (2017) and *The Kingdom of Copper* (2019). The third, *The Empire of Gold* (2020), casts a far wider net, incorporating elements from Ethiopia, Somalia, Egypt, and the Swahili coast, as well as trade networks in and around the Indian Ocean. In this book, Ali, after being exiled from Daevabad, forges alliances among the djinn kingdoms as well as with other magical beings from these regions in order to return and overthrow his father's despotic rule. His journeys have much more in common with those of *Priory* than of conventional Western medievalisms as in *Vikings* or *ASOIAF*. Ali learns truths about the world, his family, and himself that allow him to build mutually beneficial alliances even with former enemies. That is, his mobility in the world is not colonial or Orientalised and expands rather than closes off the limits of the narrative community at the centre of the epic. Through this storyline, Chakraborty delves into the complex relationships and mobilities between the various regions, bringing to popular medievalist fantasy a perspective that resonates with global Middle Ages approaches but is rarely seen outside specialist academic circles.

By centring Muslim characters and traditions, moreover, the Daevabad Trilogy pushes back against the persistent Islamophobia that underpins much of Western popular medievalism and has deep roots in medieval European culture.[178] The conventional Orientalised enemies of Western epic fantasy, from the Southrons and orcs of Sauron's armies in *The Lord of the Rings* to the enslaved eunuch Unsullied of the *ASOIAF* franchise, are racialised stereotypes of Muslim peoples that often reflect the tropes of medieval romance.[179] In other epic fantasy, including *The Priory of the Orange Tree*, Islam is erased

---

[177] Chakraborty has specified that, while Nahri 'would have grown up in a profoundly Islamic world and likely taken much of its associations and traditions as her own', she herself does not practise Islam and would not consider herself Muslim, primarily due to 'how much religion was associated with one's societal place and family'. Personal email communication with KMF, 8 September 2021.
[178] Rajabzadeh, 'The Depoliticized Saracen and Muslim Erasure'.
[179] See the previous section.

altogether, as is Judaism. The closest parallel to either of these religions is the eponymous Priory, but even that is a significant interpretive stretch, and this lacuna reflects the larger challenge of incorporating a truly global perspective into a Eurocentric fantasy text. Chakraborty's recentring of epic fantasy on Islam and in Central Asia is a counterstory to the Western genre that, in Ebony Thomas' words, develops a 'restorying of the imagination'.[180]

Islam becomes a force of connection across enormous distances, culturally significant even to those who are not themselves practitioners. Chakraborty has spoken candidly about her own background and position as a white woman who converted to Islam in her teens, and what she felt was her role as a fantasy author building on Middle Eastern history, mythology, and tradition: 'I try to hold myself accountable to fellow Muslims first, and to show respect and justice to a culture and history that I never forget isn't mine despite how much I might enjoy it.'[181] She explains that she wrote the trilogy primarily for her community of Muslim fans of science fiction and fantasy, who largely lacked satisfactory representation in the genre.[182] As an aid to Western readers who are less versed in the cultural norms of the Middle East, she includes a glossary of terms at the end of each book and has a more detailed breakdown of the universe on her website. She also keeps a frequently updated reading list of primarily nonfiction books she uses to research her novels and highlights scholarship and resources on her social media feeds.[183] For example, she tweeted on 3 June 2021 about a forthcoming edition of *The Thousand and One Nights* translated by Yasmin Seale that she had been able to access prior to its publication.[184] That the trilogy is a bestseller and was nominated for a 2021 Hugo Award speaks not just to Chakraborty's talent as a writer, but to an obvious desire on the part of readers for more diverse voices and ideas in fantasy fiction.

The Daevabad Trilogy rejects Western Orientalist stereotypes and temporal medievalisms that construct Eastern societies as both backward and static. In *Priory of the Orange Tree*, as discussed in the previous section, Western Virtudom is potentially set on the path away from religious feudalism and towards secular democratic modernity while the East, Seiiki and the Empire of Twelve Lakes remain in their pre-modern feudal and imperial political structures.

---

[180] Thomas, *The Dark Fantastic*, 163.

[181] Krishna, 'S. A. Chakraborty's the City of Brass Started Out As History Fan Fiction'.

[182] Rebecca Hankins argued more than a decade ago that a 'growing list of authors and writings are providing a critical mass of literature' in science fiction and fantasy that draws on Islam and Islamic traditions, but also points out that such literature is not necessarily 'free of bias, stereotypes, or blatant inaccuracies'. Hankins, 'Fictional Islam', 89.

[183] Chakraborty, 'Reading List'.

[184] Chakraborty (@SAChakrabooks) *Twitter*, 3 June 2021, https://twitter.com/SAChakrabooks/status/1400462238553501701.

Figure 3 Nahri e Nahid and Alizayd Al Qahtani. Digital illustration by April Damon, commissioned by S. A. Chakraborty, copyright 2020. Image appears with kind permission of the artist and author.

Even *Game of Thrones* points towards colonial modernity in the final episode when Arya says she will go 'west of Westeros' in a line that clearly refers to white colonisation of the Americas. White Western modernity is the implied future of the realms coded as white in these examples. The titles of the novels in the Daevabad Trilogy suggest a teleological increase of sovereignty – *The City of Brass*, *The Kingdom of Copper*, and *The Empire of Gold* – but the narrative ultimately rejects this. Neither protagonist who has a hereditary claim on rulership takes it up at the end of *The Empire of Gold*; indeed, both push against these claims for most of the trilogy, despite immense pressure from characters around them. The end state of Daevabad, at least for purposes of the trilogy, is a kind of constitutional council drawn from multiple classes, factions, and allegiances. The fact that Nahri and Ali (see Figure 3) are both mixed-race— which with both grapple in simultaneously empowering and traumatic fashion— is crucial to their ability to bridge previously impassable divides between tribes of djinn.[185]

The sacred city of Daevabad is the mooring at the heart of an empire, bringing traders and pilgrims as well as ambassadors from other realms to it throughout the series, and at the heart of mobilities for multiple characters in the novel.

---

[185] See, for instance, Rachel Schine's module on *Race and Blackness in Early Islamic Thought*.

It is also symbolically closed off, a centre of power where movement in and out, as well as within its walls, is rigidly circumscribed. The city and the lake that surrounds it are closed off from the rest of the world – human and djinn – by a magical border. The lake, as far as anyone in the city is aware, is cursed, though the reasons for that curse remain obscured until Ali discovers them during his journey in *The Empire of Gold*. The city, moreover, is both surrounded by enormous brass walls and strictly divided into seven quarters, echoing Suleiman's division of the djinn into six tribes, with the addition of a Daeva quarter. Keeping the tribes separate is crucial to maintaining the power of the ruling dynasty, and only an alliance between them is powerful enough to topple Ghassan Al Qahtani. The narrative is not one of nostalgic return of a rightful or even 'good' ruler, reinscribing existing power structures and securing the well-being of a 'thinning' land, as is conventional in epic fantasy.[186] Rather, it is one of social and political progress in which the removal of borders and boundaries is both literal and symbolic.

The Daevabad Trilogy is a recent, highly successful example of popular fantasy that takes up Islamic culture and history as the centre of narrative and focus of epic. Djinn and ghouls also feature in Saladin Ahmed's *Throne of the Crescent Moon* (2012) and G. Willow Wilson's *Alif the Unseen* (2012). Renée Andieh's *The Wrath & the Dawn* (2015) and *The Rose & the Dagger* (2016) draw inspiration from the frame story for *The Thousand and One Nights* for the protagonist, Shahrzad, as well as stories of blood curses and magic spells. More grounded in a specific historical period is Guy Gavriel Kay's *The Lions of Al-Rassan* (1995), set in an alternate version of al-Andalus on the cusp of invasion from the (pseudo-Christian) north. All of these examples, like the Daevabad Trilogy, suggest alternate medievalist mobilities and intentionally centre non-Christian perspectives. While elements of Orientalism and stereotyping are found in some such works, the recentring of fantasy to make a conventional other the narrative self is a crucial part of the process of restorying that resists the temporal medievalism applied to Islam and to Muslim peoples, cultures, and societies by the West.[187]

Counterstories and alternate mobilities have long been part of fiction emerging from Asia and the Asian diaspora, but the past several years have seen a flourishing of medievalist fantasy in particular. Tasha Suri's *Books of Ambha* (2018–19) and Roshani Chokshi's *Star-Touched* (2016–17) duologies create immersive fantasy worlds grounded in the history and culture of different parts of India. Chokshi's two novels also draw on elements from Greek mythology, specifically the tale of Hades and Persephone, and she has discussed her mixed-race and mixed-religious

---

[186] Clute, 'Thinning'.   [187] Swank, 'The Arabian Nights in 21st-Century Fantasy Fiction'.

background in interviews.[188] Suri, in the meantime, aims to deconstruct not just assumptions about South Asian culture, but also about the complexities of gender within that culture, and her books often feature queer characters and relationships. Moving further eastward, Nghi Vo's novellas *The Empress of Salt and Fortune* (2020) and *When the Tiger Came Down the Mountain* (2020), similarly evoke a lost, mythological version of Imperial China. *Netflix*'s South Korean production *Kingdom* (2019–), which currently has two seasons and is set during the late sixteenth-century Japanese invasion of Korea, is an interesting example because it highlights the capacity of international streaming services to bring national productions to a global audience. These works are arguably part of an emerging process of global medievalism in contemporary popular culture which expands the geographic scope of 'medieval'. While there has been a trend in fantasy since the late twentieth century of 'creation of settings that are pre-modern but not European', the past five years or so have seen increased representation of authors and creators whose own backgrounds and/or beliefs connect to the material on which they draw.[189]

Decolonising Arthuriana

The Arthurian Extended Universe (AEU) comprises the enormous body of work surrounding the legendary King Arthur and his knights of the Round Table – not just prose and poetry, but drama, film, music, visual art, material culture (e.g. fifteenth-century Burgundian tournaments with an Arthurian theme), modern fan practices (e.g. Arthurian-themed Renaissance faires), and so forth. Much like the enormous, franchise-driven fandoms of the early twenty-first century, the texts within this universe are consciously aware of one another and often interconnect in unexpected ways. Readers are assumed to have a basic knowledge of the characters as, for instance, in Marie de France's twelfth-century lai *Lanval*, where the titular character is an unknown knight trying to win favour in Arthur's court; or the fourteenth-century *Roman de Silence*, which features Merlin as a *deus ex machina* with no explanation for why he is there. Built into the fabric of Arthur's legend as far back as the twelfth century is the promise of his return – *rex quondam, rex futurus*, the once and future king. But it is ultimately a tragic story bookended by grief, betrayal, and broken families. There is no sense that one version is any more valid or authoritative than another; in fact, many claim to be translating allegedly lost older texts, only some of which can be confirmed to have existed at all. Characters die, return to life, appear, and disappear at random for bouts of madness in the woods; what is

---

[188] Charaiportra, 'Roshani Chokshi Is Writing for Second-Gen Kids Like Her'.
[189] Young, *Race and Popular Fantasy Literature*, 140.

important is that it is very much a shared universe, agreed-upon between authors and readers. In this, the AEU shares many commonalities with another popular medieval fantasy figure, Robin Hood. As Stephen Knight has observed, stories of Robin Hood evoke what he calls a rhizomatic structure, where 'the coherent determinants of time, place, class and power, as well as their servants in terms of literary tradition, operate only in a casual, not causal, way'.[190]

As for the myth of Camelot, it is, of course, central not just to English nationalism, but to white supremacy, as Andrew Elliot and Wen Chuan Kao have demonstrated.[191] This is not the limit of its capacities for exploring 'power in the real world', as Knight puts it, however.[192] The AEU transcends geographic and linguistic borders, drawing from and in turn influencing traditions in France, Italy, Spain, Scandinavia, Burgundy, the German principalities, and some more far-flung places than that. Mobilities in the AEU are complicated, as is temporality. While some of the locations (London, Brittany, Ireland, Rome, Constantinople) map onto the realities of medieval Europe, there are twice as many imagined locales, legendary kingdoms, and paths between the legendary realm and the real world. As for temporality, it is a world forever poised between medieval and modern, *quondam* and *futurus*. Some Arthurian works nod to the legend's roots in stories of a warlord in the waning years of the Roman Empire, while others fashion Arthur's court as a reflection of the one in which they were produced. In the longer prose romances of the Vulgate Cycle and Thomas Malory's *Morte D'Arthur*, time dilates and shifts and events are sometimes presented out of order, in flashback, or as proleptic prophecy. Drenched in nostalgia, the legend reaches forever backward to a time of magic and chivalry; it is, on some level, the heart of modern medievalism. Arthur, for all his flaws and the substantial variation in ideological positions espoused in the vast range of texts, is always perceived to be on the side of good. Arthurian medievalism encompasses imperial and colonial perspectives, but also postcolonial resistance and alternative positions.[193] Arthuriana is, in short,

---

[190] Knight, *Reading Robin Hood*, 237.

[191] The far-right, fascist British National Party, for example, designed its 'Camp Excalibur as a 'family-friendly get away to instil in its members a sense of the British past' as both mythical and urgently present and in need of defending. Elliott, *Medievalism, Politics and Mass Media*, 180. As Wen-Chuan Kao observes in an article about racial violence and Kazuo Ishiguro's *The Buried Giant*, 'a distorted and ill-informed notion of the past has … authorized some … to defend the Arthurian canon' from both himself and Ishiguro as 'embodiment[s] of the racial other'. Kao, 'The Fragile Giant', 10. For Nazism and Arthuriana, see Shichtman and Finke, 'Exegetical History'.

[192] Knight, *Arthurian Literature and Society*, xiv.

[193] Lynch, 'Post-colonial Studies'; for Arthuriana in Japan, see Momma, 'Medievalism–Colonialism–Orientalism'; for the use of Arthurian tropes in the making of nineteenth-century Puerto Rican identity, see Otaño Gracia, 'Broken Dreams'. For examples of

full of potential for counterstorytelling and resistant, transformative reading and restorying.

Twenty-first-century popular culture retellings include more or less medievalist versions from pseudo-historical tales set towards the end of the Roman Empire – that is, Antoine Fuqua's *King Arthur* (2004) to Guy Ritchie's violent fantasy *King Arthur: Legend of the Sword* (2017) and the BBC's young adult fantasy series *Merlin* (2008–12).[194] The restorying of Arthurian legends from feminist perspectives has been reasonably common since at least the publication of Marion Zimmer Bradley's *The Mists of Avalon* (1983), particularly in novels and Arthuriana aimed at young people, but *Merlin* offered a potential, if not quite realised, challenge to the conventional whiteness of even these modern retellings with the casting of Afro-Guyanese actress Angel Coulby as Guinevere.[195] Unfortunately, as Thomas addresses in detail, Coulby dealt with significant backlash and the writers and showrunners behind *Merlin* chose to short-change her character.[196] More recently, Arthuriana has been increasingly reimagined from the perspectives of groups conventionally 'endarkened', to borrow Thomas' term, by white Western patriarchal medievalism in works that reimagine medieval pasts and medievalist stories and reposition the Arthurian cycle in the present and future.

For instance, Saladin Ahmed's 2013 short story 'Without Faith, without Law, without Joy' is a rewriting of Edmund Spenser's epic poem *The Faerie Queene* (*c.*1595, itself a tangential text within the Arthurian universe) from the perspective of its 'Saracen' enemies. Ahmed places the three Muslim brothers killed by Redcrosse at the centre of Spenser's epic, 'restorying perspective', in Thomas' terms, to 'redefine and renarrativize the world'.[197] The narrator is forced to watch the all-powerful Redcrosse strike down both of his elder brothers after having been sucked into Spenser's medievalist world from the streets of Damascus, and spends most of the story unable to remember his or their true names. His triumph is not in surviving, but in remembering the truth beneath Spenser's mythology, that 'I am Abdul Wadud, the Servant of God the Loving'.[198] The centring of the 'enemy other' perspective in an originally white Christian crusader medievalist

---

engagements with medieval Arthuriana through postcolonial theory, see Finke and Shichtman, *King Arthur and the Myth of History*; Ingham, *Sovereign Fantasies*; Warren, 'Making Contact'.

[194] On Arthuriana in popular culture, see Sklar and Hoffman, *King Arthur in Popular Culture*.

[195] On twentieth-century popular fiction, see Howey, *Rewriting the Women of Camelot*. On recent Arthuriana for young people, see, for example, Bradford and Hutton, 'Female Protagonists in Arthurian Television for the Young'; Tolhurst, 'Helping Girls to Be Heroic?'.

[196] Thomas, *The Dark Fantastic*, 65–106. On actors of colour in Arthuriana more broadly, see Wymer, 'A Quest for the Black Knight'.

[197] Thomas, *The Dark Fantastic*, 160–1. Thomas quotes Xie, 'Rethinking the Identity of Cultural Otherness'.

[198] Ahmed, 'Without Faith, without Law, without Joy', 340.

narrative is a powerful example of counterstorytelling that reveals ideological assumptions and exclusions enacted by and through Spenser's epic poem and the broader story of medievalism of which it is part.

Tracy Deonn's *Legendborn* (2020), the first half of a duology that will conclude with *Bloodmarked* in late 2022, asks the question so many modern Arthurian retellings, from *Merlin* to *The Kingsmen*, take for granted – *do* we want Arthur to return? Why are we so invested in this singular, mythological figure? What if the world order for which he stands is a corrupted one that must be destroyed and rebuilt? The novel's strong anti-racist stance and its incisive reading of a foundational medieval mythos illustrate a way to incorporate those flawed but deeply loved medieval topics into larger conversations about race, representation, and white supremacy. In a similar vein, the short story collection *Sword Stone Table* (2021), edited by Swapna Krishna and Jenn Northington, brings together an impressive list of authors to produce what they call 'bent' retellings of the Arthurian legend – transformative fictions that interrogate specific aspects of Arthuriana, primarily focussed on race, gender, and sexuality. *Once & Future* (2019) and *Sword in the Stars* (2020), by Amy Rose Capetta and Cori McCarthy, combine science fiction, medievalism, and metanarrative to place queer characters of colour at the centre of the Arthurian cycle, reimagining the meaning and significance of the hero's quest.

Legendborn appears, on the surface, to fall into the much-derided genre of paranormal young adult fiction, pitting its sixteen-year-old protagonist against a powerful secret society as she searches for the truth about her mother's sudden death and grapples with supernatural abilities she cannot explain. Attentive readers can spot the Arthurian references as early as the second chapter, but it is not until about halfway through the novel that it transforms into a radical revisioning of the Arthurian mythos that foregrounds and interrogates the whiteness at its core. Deonn 'restories' time, place and identity in the Arthurian mythos by placing the narrative in the American South, in the present day, with a teenaged Black girl as the protagonist. This restorying enables striking counterstorytelling that challenges the racial logics on which spatial medievalism depends; after all, as Deonn has argued in a separate essay for *Tor*, all Arthuriana is ultimately 'fanfic about who gets to be legendary'.[199]

As Thomas demonstrates through her analysis of major young adult franchises, 'a person of colour – or even a *character of colour* – faces dire consequences when he or she steps outside of his or her assigned place, or flips the script in any way'.[200] Central to *Legendborn*'s project is the setting – the University of North Carolina (UNC) at Chapel Hill. As of this writing, the

---

[199] See Deonn, 'Every King Arthur Retelling'.   [200] Thomas, *The Dark Fantastic*, 61.

university has appeared in the news several times for incidents and controversies clearly rooted in white supremacy, most notably the tenure denial of Nikole Hannah-Jones, founder of the Pulitzer-winning 1619 Project, who subsequently joined the school of journalism at the historically black Howard University. None of this had happened at the time of *Legendborn*'s publication, but the scenes between Bree and white authority figures ring uncomfortably true.[201] The novel foregrounds the implication of classicism and medievalism very early on. Bree learns the secret societies at UNC are named 'the Gorgons, the Golden Fleece, the Stygians, the Valkyries, and the Round Table'.[202] A few pages later, she recalls a school trip to the North Carolina state capitol, with its 'gorgeous Greek revival architecture', observing that 'those folks never thought *I'd* be strolling the halls, walking around thinking about how their ghosts would kick me out if they could'.[203] While Bree remains, for better or worse, tied to this physical location, the journey she undergoes is one that unlocks temporal rather than geographical mobilities, bringing her into contact with not just the Arthurian world, but her own buried past (see Figure 4).

The Order of the Round Table in *Legendborn* encapsulates Geraldine Heng's characterisation of an 'elite, exclusive, self-serving, privileged, male fraternity of knights, imagined as White-Caucasian and Christian'.[204] It is a group formed around the direct descendants of King Arthur and his chief knights; Arthur and his knights can possess their 'Scion' in times of danger from an evil otherworld of demons. The Order is not limited to UNC Chapel Hill, but has members and acolytes in the halls of political and commercial power, as well as arrangements with university and local authorities, including the police. Their 'cover' as a college fraternity 'is perfect', not only because of the exclusivity and secrecy that surrounds such organisations, but because of the power and privilege associated with them, particularly with traditionally white fraternities.[205] They are metonymic, in the novel and arguably also in reality, for white racial privilege.

Deonn places Bree within the confluence of the two competing philosophies of magic use at work in her novel. First introduced is the idea of *aether*, a force that can be manipulated in various ways (to heal, to wound, to shapeshift, to modify memories, etc.), and that only some people can see. The Order of the Round Table is strictly hierarchical in the familiar tradition of the Oxford School of fantasy literature, but seeing it through the eyes of a Black protagonist

---

[201] We recall here the direct connection Thomas draws between the world of the imagination and political and social realities.

[202] Deonn, *Legendborn*, 73.

[203] Deonn, *Legendborn*, 75. See also Monteiro, 'Power Structures' for an encapsulation of how architecture and white supremacy operate together, particularly in the southern United States.

[204] Heng, 'An Arthurian Empire of Magic', 130.   [205] Deonn, *Legendborn*, 74.

Figure 4 Bree Matthews. Digital illustration by Ace Artemis, copyright 2021. Image appears with kind permission of the artist.

allows the reader to question why it is so familiar. 'Oxford School fantasy', according to Cecire, aims 'to re-enchant the world by rehabilitating forms, narratives, and belief systems that identify the potential for magic in everyday life, and offer them to the public as alternatives to a discourse of disenchantment'.[206] In addition to the wonder at the secrets she uncovers, Bree carries a deep and well-earned suspicion of the entire system that ultimately pays off for both her and the reader when it becomes clear that the Order of the Round Table is, like its Arthurian precedent, rooted in white supremacist ideology and deeply corrupt.

Alongside her nascent interest in *aether*, Bree is introduced to a second philosophy of magic, this one called *root*. The name evokes not a force for unseen control, but a living connection – in this case, to ancestry, bloodlines, and

---

[206] Cecire, *Re-enchanted*, 14.

(counter)stories. *Root* works through collaboration and sharing of power, in contrast to the mastery and control of *aether*; the two systems are anathema to their different users. It is no coincidence that all the users of *root* Bree encounters are women of colour, specifically Black women who, at the very least, understand Bree's intersectional dilemma, if not share it. This magical practice grounded in connection and consent echoes the kind of alternative geographies that Katherine McKittrick describes in *Demonic Grounds* – 'genealogically wrapped up in the historical spatial unrepresentability of black femininity' – and it is significant that many of these scenes take place in the burial ground dedicated to enslaved people at UNC.[207] Over the course of the novel, Deonn employs a series of impressionistic flashbacks as Bree follows the source of *root* further back in time to solve the enigma of her mother's death and to find the explanation for her powers. This concept, particularly within a medievalist text like *Legendborn*, calls back to Knight's rhizomatic structure of storytelling discussed earlier.

What makes the denouement satisfying is not just that King Arthur is reincarnated as a Black woman (although that is well worth celebrating), but the carefully woven destruction of the prior white supremacist structure that brought her into being in the first place. Bree discovers, in a striking chapter written not in prose but in free verse, that her enslaved ancestor Vera was raped by a man from the Davis family and, when trying to escape, called upon the *root* to protect her. When she drew on the power of her ancestors, so too did her unborn child, and she unknowingly bound herself and her descendants to Arthur's line.

> They hear her. Their voices rise up from the earth.
> Up through her wound and into her veins
> and directly into her soul.
> *'Bound to your blood?'*
> She gasps. The dogs are at the creek. Tears drop into the dirt.
> "Yes, please! Bound to my blood!"
> *'A price.'* The voices sigh, sad and heavy.
> *'One daughter at a time, for all time.'*
> "Bind us to it!" she cries.[208]

Deonn deliberately slows the narrative to force the reader into this moment with Bree, this moment where temporality dissolves and she lives multiple lives at once. History is no longer relegated to dust, but horribly, traumatically, alive – it is, in a sense, McKittrick's demonic grounds made manifest, the combined weight of innumerable generations collapsing down upon Bree. It is also, however, the source of her power, and she takes control of that power when

---

[207] McKittrick, *Demonic Grounds*, xxv.   [208] Deonn, *Legendborn*, 467–8.

the narrative restarts in the subsequent chapter, setting the stage for the story's continuation in *Bloodmarked*.

Davis' rape of Vera is a violent assertion of white masculine power, parallel to the violence of Vikings analysed in the 'Medieval Mobilities' section, but *Legendborn* follows the logic of global medievalism. It rejects white racial gendered assumptions about descent that structure the spatial medievalisms of settler colonies. White Western medievalisms work to legitimise claims of sovereignty in territories that white people have taken possession of through violence. The white Davis family literally loses sovereignty – its men unknowingly cease being the hereditary 'Scion' of King Arthur – through the rape of Vera. That they retain the *social* power and status of being presumed to still be the scions highlights the social construction of race and its function of maintaining white power and privilege. Bree's mobilities in the narrative are limited to the surrounds of the university, but mooring the novel there enables its deconstructive rejection of the racial logics that structure the colonial movement of medievalism. *Legendborn* thus reveals the false assumptions and contradictions inherent not only in spatial medievalisms, but in white racial medievalisms through this powerfully deconstructive counterstorytelling.

Legendborn therefore reclaims the Arthurian myth while offering a searing coming-of-age story very much in line with its medieval forbearers. The temptations Bree faces along the way would feel familiar to the eponymous hero of *Sir Gawain and the Green Knight*, and while it is likely coincidental that David Lowery's film adaptation of that poem was originally intended to be released the same year as *Legendborn*'s publication, the subsequent centring of South Asian actor Dev Patel as Gawain has raised a variety of questions about the nature of the AEU, as well as the place of characters of colour within that universe.[209]

Amy Rose Capetta and Cori McCarthy's *Once and Future* (2019) and *Sword in the Stars* (2020) duology is also young adult, and is animated by similar questions. It melds Arthurian lore with science fiction, reincarnating Arthur as a young queer person, Ari, from an Arabic background born into a galactic capitalist empire. Ari's friends, named for various Arthurian figures (Percival, Guinevere, Kai, etc.) are variously queer and racially and culturally diverse; only Kai is the white, cisgendered heterosexual male conventionally at the centre of the AEU. They are accompanied in their struggles with the ruling Mercer corporation by Merlin, who is aging backwards as imagined in

---

[209] See Deonn, 'Every King Arthur Retelling'; also issue 31.2 of *Arthuriana*, edited by Richard Sevère, and titled *Race, Equity, and Justice in Arthurian Studies*. For medieval literature and/as fanfiction, see Finn, 'Conversations in the Margins'; Nielsen, 'Christine de Pizan's The Book of the City of Ladies As Reclamatory Fan Work'; Wilson, 'Full-Body Reading'.

T. H. White's *Once and Future King* (1958) and in his teen and childhood years
in the duology. The novels move between the science fictional future and
an imagined past which places the beginning of the Arthurian cycle of
reincarnation – and its attendant repeated story of heroic failure – in the 'Anglo-
Saxon' period of England's history in a move that resonates powerfully with the
white racial imaginings of much of colonial medievalism.[210] It rejects the
habitual whiteness of medievalist narratives: Merlin says, 'I'd even grown
used to the notion that people of colour were not featured in this era of
European history. I don't know who started *that* lie, but Hollywood was quite
talented at spreading it.'[211]

The duology is metafictional and asserts the power of stories and restorying:
Merlin 'knew from deep personal experience playing a role in one of the most
enduring legends in Western history, that stories were never just a string of
pretty words . . . They climbed inside your head, reordered things, tore up parts
of you by the roots and planted new ideas'.[212] It is also a fundamental rejection
of the individualist masculine hero's quest, as theorised by Joseph Campbell,
which has been repeated through forty-two reincarnations of Arthur; all of
whom have failed to unite humanity and achieve the promise of Camelot. Ari,
Merlin, and their friends 'reimagine the very stories themselves', understanding
the narrative core of white masculine Arthuriana as rooted in injustice and
exclusion and in need of rewriting; they perform this restorying by prioritising
connection, love, and equality, much as Deonn emphasises the importance of
found families and the impact of generational trauma in *Legendborn*.

These questions are also central to the 2021 story collection *Sword Stone
Table*, edited by Swapna Krishna and Jenn Northington.[213] Imagined in three
sections – 'Once', 'Present', and 'Future' – the collection leans into temporal
mobilities in its approach and geographical mobilities in its contributors, many
of whom identify as BIPOC. The very first story of the 'Once' section, 'The
Once and Future Qadi' by Ausma Zehenat Khan, drops the Arthurian universe
into a network of global mobilities by introducing the character of Yusuf, the
titular Qadi of Córdoba who has been asked by the king of the Franks to
'adjudicate in the matter of his queen's fidelity'.[214] The familiar characters of
Arthur, Guinevere, and Lancelot are made strange through Yusuf's gaze, the
well-known love triangle of king, queen, and knight given new and interesting
resonance with the backdrop of Islamic rather than Christian law. For instance,
at one point, Guinevere's story is put in conversation with the accusation of

---

[210] Capetta and McCarthy, *Sword in the Stars*, 279.
[211] Capetta and McCarthy, *Sword in the Stars*, 22.
[212] Capetta and McCarthy, *Sword in the Stars*, 343–4.
[213] Krishna and Northington, *Sword Stone Table*.   [214] Khan, 'The Once and Future Qadi', 3.

adultery brought against the Prophet Muhammad's wife Aisha in sura An-Nur of the Qur'an, and there are a number of instances when members of Arthur's court, including Guinevere herself, attempt to stereotype or otherwise racialise the perceived interloper. Similarly, Nisi Shawl's story, 'I Being Young and Foolish', reimagines the enchantress Nimue as Nia, a magic user from what is now Uganda, and traces her evolving relationship with Merlin and Arthur through the lens of Central African tradition. In such stories, which reposition characters and perspectives away from the conventions of white medievalism, we can see postcolonial strategies of appropriation that are characteristic of global medievalism.[215] They also foreground the globality of the medieval world through the mobility of the central characters.

The first two sections are significantly longer than the third, comprising stories with medievalist settings ('Once') and contemporary settings ('Present'). The 'Present' and 'Future' sections of *Sword Stone Table* operate along the lines of alternate universe fanfiction, transposing characters and moments into other times and places in ways that resonate with Deonn and Capetta and McCarthy's young adult novels. Such stories find in Arthuriana, 'not just a self-contained text, but a series of generative potentialities'.[216] These potentialities apply across genres as well as time periods and Arthurian themes resonate where one may not expect them. Matthew Vernon, for example, finds 'phantasmal' connections to the Arthurian universe in N. K. Jemisin's urban fantasy novel *The City We Became* (2020), particularly in conversation with Kazuo Ishiguro's more explicitly Arthurian novel *The Buried Giant* (2015).

When the trailer for David Lowery's film *The Green Knight*, starring Dev Patel, dropped in summer 2020, the level of excitement amongst South Asian bloggers, critics, academics, and fans was undeniable. This was perceived as not simply a matter of 'colour-blind casting', but colour-conscious casting and the deliberate restorying of fourteenth century source material.[217] As we briefly discuss in the conclusion, the film itself does not quite live up to that promise, but it nonetheless continues the optimistic trend of opening up not just the setting of the Middle Ages, but its canonical texts for reinterpretation and transformation.

Restorying Medievalism

Arthuriana, with its multiplicity of tales and habit of reflecting 'power in the real world', can be considered a microcosm of medievalism.[218] According to

---

[215] On appropriation as a postcolonial strategy, see Ashcroft, Griffiths, and Tiffin, *The Empire Writes Back*, 58–76.

[216] Finn and McCall, 'Exit, Pursued by a Fan', 41.

[217] For colour-blind casting and its problems, see Thompson, *Passing Strange*.

[218] Knight, *Arthurian Literature and Society*, xiv.

Thomas, 'not only does the recurring popularity of Camelot demonstrate the adaptability of a set of tales popular for more than a millennium, it also provides room for those in a multicultural Britain – and, because the program was exported, a multicultural world – to identify with Arthurian legend, instead of feeling excluded and alienated from it'.[219] The medieval past was associated with white racism, colonialism, and imperialism through a still ongoing process of storytelling that privileges a narrative core that supports real-world power structures and ideologies. As the variety of texts – Arthurian and otherwise – discussed in this section demonstrate, counterstorytelling and restorying are powerful tools for resisting hegemonic positions and for imagining, and asserting the inherent value of, alternatives. Global medievalism as a process is an emerging force in contemporary popular culture.

---

[219] Thomas, *The Dark Fantastic*, 105.

Coda: Global Medievalism Redux

'Restorying the imagination itself' opens up 'infinite narrative possibilities'.[220] Global medievalism depends on plurality to dispute and disrupt the power of the core narrative of white Western medievalism that has been historically dominant for centuries, although not without being actively resisted. No single narrative in any genre or medium of popular culture marks a global medievalist state as having been achieved. Multiplicity and connections feature centrally in the works that engage in global medievalist storytelling that we have analysed in this Element: from the root magic system of *Legendborn*, to the Inuit world view that emphasises human connection to the Land in *Skraelings*; the alliances Ali makes in the Daevabad Trilogy; the plurality of stories, perspectives, and identities in global Arthuriana; to the world-risk society of *Priory*. Networks overcome singularity in these texts, symbolising the nature of global medievalism and its capacity to reimagine the past, present, and future.

As we stressed in the introduction, this Element is intended to start conversations about global medievalism in popular culture. As we have presented this research, we have fielded questions about potential global medievalisms in Turkey, India, China, Korea, and Central Africa, and it is our hope that some of these will appear later in the series, with contributors whose expertise in those topics can be amplified. But we will address what may seem a strange omission from an introductory work on global popular medievalism: that of historical fiction novels.

Popular historical fiction, even when written about people who have been excluded from the archives and received medievalist (or other) narratives, has a strong generic adherence to discourses of 'historical authenticity'. It is almost impossible to find an historical fiction text that does not engage with this discourse in its paratexts, from authors' notes to book reviews and fan discussions.

Historical fiction can fill in the gaps of known events or mess about with details of who died in which battle, but in its popular iterations in particular, if a text moves outside teleological white Western history, it stops being considered – and therefore sold and read – as 'authentic'. One or two characters of colour might appear, passing through Europe as traders or diplomats as in *The Thirteenth Warrior*, or in a 'colour-blind' casting that does not alter the medievalist narrative or metanarratives as in the casting of Black actress Sophie

---

[220] Thomas, *The Dark Fantastic*, 163–4.

Okonedo as Queen Margaret of Anjou in the BBC's 2013 adaptation of Shakespeare's *Henry VI*, which generated significant racist backlash. But the sweep of history, challenges to teleological modernity that depend on white Western temporality as Heng and Ramey characterise it, do not fit with the conventions, textual and otherwise, of the genre. The dominant restorying in popular medievalist historical fiction is centred on gender – the telling of white women's stories – in narratives that almost without exception do not fit our conception of global medievalism.[221]

Global medievalism is an ongoing process of retelling the Middle Ages that disputes centuries' worth of hegemonic medievalism. It is not solely interested in creating versions of the past that represent a 'global Middle Ages', although that is part of its overall project. Global medievalism incorporates both counter-storytelling and restorying. Counterstorytelling, for our purposes, means the creation of narratives (fictional and metafictional) that dispute the story of the bounded European Middle Ages that 'went global' through imperialism and colonialism. Restorying is the reimagination of medievalism and the identities that can be constructed through it by shifting 'time, place, identity, perspective, mode and metanarratives', often in combination.[222] Counterstorytelling and restorying overlap, almost without exception, in any given example of global medievalism. The sections on Viking fictions and fantasy epics illustrate both the limitations of the current Eurocentric Middle Ages and the potentialities for counterstorytelling already available, before turning to restorying in the contemporary fantasy genre for the final section.

The two main strategies of global medievalism are deconstruction and decentring; these broadly align with counterstorytelling and restorying, respectively. The deconstructive mode works with and within white Western medievalism and the ideologies it supports (racial, colonial, patriarchal, heterosexist) to reveal their underlying assumptions and contradictions. This often manifests in popular culture by subverting genre conventions, as in *The Priory of the Orange Tree*. The decentring mode either makes Europe, its people, and their perspectives one of several narrative centres, or altogether peripheral to the narrative. It does not use a layer of 'diversity' markers (e.g. cultural references, somatic features of characters) over a structurally white Western text to 'just paint 'em brown', as N. K. Jemisin has observed of conventional fantasy, but rather challenges Eurocentric logics and ideologies by centring alternatives.[223] The Daevabad Trilogy, for example, centres its cultural geography on the

---

[221] Examples include the novels of Philippa Gregory, Karen Brooks' *The Good Wife of Bath*, and even Lauren Groff's *The Matrix*, despite its marketing as literary rather than popular fiction.

[222] Thomas, *The Dark Fantastic*, 159.

[223] Jemisin, 'Identity Should Always Be Part of the Gameplay'.

Middle East and Islam, while *Skraelings: Clashes in the Old Arctic* restories a 'first-contact' narrative from the perspective of a conventionally othered people, the Inuit. These two strategies almost without exception work together in any given example of global medievalist storytelling.

Both modes have limitations, particularly when the narrative focus of an imagined world is still a version of 'the West'. *The Priory of the Orange Tree* engages in both deconstruction and decentring with its subversion of fantasy cultural geography and narrative structure, but is nonetheless limited by its refusal to engage more than superficially with Orientalist stereotypes. David Lowery's *The Green Knight* (2021) similarly offered an array of possibilities in its casting not just of Dev Patel, but also Sarita Choudhury as Morgan le Fay, and its deliberate juxtaposition of fourteenth-, sixteenth-, and nineteenth-century visual notes and iconographies before foreclosing on all of these in a disappointingly nihilistic ending that emphasised 'gritty' rather than global medievalism. This is in spite of the addition of several extra-textual female characters, whose presence, Usha Vishnuvajjala argues, 'makes literal the implied violence against women in many Arthurian texts'.[224] Unlike the poem on which it is based, which ends with Gawain's return to Camelot as he grapples with his choices and their consequences, the film looks forward – or, rather, ponders whether it ought to look forward. Rather than using Patel and Choudhury's presence to say something new about the Arthurian universe and its place within a larger world, also hinted in the film's lushly atmospheric visuals, Lowery sidesteps any of that potential significance in favour of yet another alienated man. At least this time he's not white.

---

[224] Vishnuvajjala, 'Gender, Adaptation, and the Future in David Lowery's *The Green Knight*'.

Bibliography

Ahmed, Saladin. 'Is "Game of Thrones" Too White?', *Salon.com*. 1 April 2012. www.salon.com/2012/04/01/is_game_of_thrones_too_white.

'Without Faith, without Law, without Joy', in Melissa Marr and Tim Pratt (eds.), *Rags & Bones: New Twists on Timeless Tales* (New York: Little Brown, 2013), 327–41.

Alexander, Michael. *Medievalism: The Middle Ages in Modern England* (New Haven, CT: Yale University Press, 2007).

Altschul, Nadia R. *Geographies of Philological Knowledge: Postcoloniality and the Transatlantic National Epic* (Chicago: University of Chicago Press, 2012).

'Medievalism and the Contemporaneity of the Medieval in Postcolonial Brazil', *Studies in Medievalism* 24 (2015): 139–54.

Andrews, Tarren. 'Indigenous Futures and Medieval Pasts: An Introduction', *English Language Notes* 58.2 (2020): 1–17. https://doi.org/10.1215/00138282-8557777.

Ashcroft, Bill, Gareth Griffiths, and Helen Tiffin. *The Empire Writes Back* (London: Routledge, 2002).

Balfe, Myles. 'Incredible Geographies? Orientalism and Genre Fantasy', *Social and Cultural Geography* 5.1 (2004): 75–90.

Banivanua Mar, Tracey. *Decolonisation and the Pacific: Indigenous Globalisation and the Ends of Empire* (Cambridge: Cambridge University Press, 2016).

Barnes, Geraldine. 'Nostalgia, Medievalism and the Vínland Voyages', *postmedieval* 2.2 (2011): 141–54. https://doi.org/10.1057/pmed.2011.2.

Viking America: The First Millennium (Cambridge: D. S. Brewer, 2001).

Barrington, Candace. 'Global Medievalism and Translation', in Louise D'Arcens (ed.), *The Cambridge Companion to Medievalism* (Cambridge: Cambridge University Press, 2016), 180–95.

Beck, Ulrich. *World Risk Society* (New York: Wiley-Blackwell, 1999).

Benioff, David, and D. B. Weiss. *Game of Thrones* Season 8, Episode 3 'The Long Night', dir. Miguel Sapochnik (HBO, 2019).

Bernárdez, Sara González. 'The Heroine's Journey: Epic Fantasy and Female Representation in Samantha Shannon's *The Priory of the Orange Tree* (2019)', in Lourdes López Ropero, Sara Prieto García-Cañedo, and José Antonio Sánchez Fajardo (eds.), *Thresholds and Ways Forward in English Studies* (Alicante, Spain Publicaciones de la Universidad de Alicante, 2021), 92–100.

Berzock, Kathleen Bickford. *Caravans of Gold, Fragments in Time: Art, Culture, and Exchange across Medieval Saharan Africa* (Princeton, NJ: Princeton University Press, 2019).

Bradford, Clare, and Rebecca Hutton. 'Female Protagonists in Arthurian Television for the Young: Gendering Camelot', in Helen Young (ed.), *The Middle Ages in Popular Culture: Medievalism, Genre, and Identity* (Amherst, NY: Cambria Press, 2015), 11–32.

Campbell, Gordon. *Norse America: The Story of a Founding Myth* (Oxford: Oxford University Press, 2021).

Cantor, Norman F. *Inventing the Middle Ages: The Lives, Works, and Ideas of the Twentieth Century* (New York: Quill, 1991).

Capetta, Amy Rose, and Cori McCarthy. *Once & Future* (New York: Little, Brown, 2019).

Sword in the Stars: A Once & Future Novel (New York: Little, Brown, 2021).

Carroll, Shiloh. 'Barbarian Colonizers and Post-colonialism in Westeros and Britain', in Brian Pavlac and Elizabeth Lott (eds.), *Game of Thrones versus History: Written in Blood* (Malden, MA: Wiley-Blackwell, 2017), 73–84.

Medievalism in A Song of Ice and Fire *and* Game of Thrones (Cambridge: D. S. Brewer, 2018).

Castle, Tammy, and Tara Parsons. 'Vigilante or Viking? Contesting the Mediated Constructions of Soldiers of Odin Norge', *Crime, Media, Culture* 15.1 (2019): 47–66. https://doi.org/10.1177/1741659017731479.

Cecire, Maria Sachiko. 'Medievalism, Popular Culture and National Identity in Children's Fantasy Literature', *Studies in Ethnicity and Nationalism* 9.3 (2009): 395–409. https://doi.org/10.1111/j.1754-9469.2009.01055.x.

Re-enchanted: The Rise of Children's Fantasy Literature in the Twentieth Century (Minneapolis: University of Minnesota Press, 2019).

Chadwick, Eleanor. 'Fantasizing History: Anachronism, Creative License and the Re-emergence of an Early Language of Storytelling', in Paul Hardwick and Kate Lister (eds.), Vikings *and the Vikings: Essays on Television's History Channel Series* (Jefferson, NC: McFarland, 2019), 36–58.

Chakraborty, Shannon A. *The City of Brass* (London: HarperCollins, 2017).

The Empire of Gold (London: HarperCollins, 2020).

The Kingdom of Copper (London: HarperCollins, 2019).

'Reading List', www.sachakraborty.com/reading-list.html.

Charaiportra, Sona. 'Roshani Chokshi Is Writing for Second-Gen Kids Like Her', *Bustle*. 5 April 2017. www.bustle.com/p/a-crown-of-wishes-author-roshani-chokshi-is-writing-for-second-generation-kids-like-her-49241.

Clinton, Hillary Rodham. 'Preface', in William W. Fitzhugh (ed.), *Vikings: The North Atlantic Saga* (Washington, DC: Smithsonian, 2000), 9–10.

Clunies Ross, Margaret. *The Norse Muse in Britain: 1750–1820* (Trieste: Parnasso, 1998).

Clunies Ross, Margaret, and Lars Lonnröth. 'The Norse Muse: Report from an International Research Project', *Alvíssmál* 9.1999 (1999): 3–28.

Clute, John. 'Thinning', *Encyclopedia of Fantasy*. John Clute and John Grant (eds.). 1997. http://sf-encyclopedia.uk/fe.php?nm=thinning.

Crang, Mike. *Cultural Geography* (London: Routledge, 1998).

Crother, Lane. *Globalization and American Popular Culture*, 2nd ed. (Lanham, MD: Rowman & Littlefield, 2010).

D'Arcens, Louise. *Old Songs in the Timeless Land: Medievalism in Australian Literature 1840–1910* (Turnhout: Brepols, 2011).

World Medievalism: The Middle Ages in Modern Textual Culture (Oxford: Oxford University Press, 2021).

D'Arcens, Louise, and Andrew Lynch (eds.) *International Medievalism and Popular Culture* (Amherst, NY: Cambria Press, 2014).

'Introduction: The Medieval, the International, the Popular', in Louise D'Arcens and Andrew Lynch (eds.), *International Medievalism and Popular Culture* (Amherst, NY: Cambria Press, 2014), xi–xxx.

D'Arcens, Louise, Andrew Lynch, and Stephanie Trigg. 'Medievalism, Nationalism, Colonialism: Introduction', *Australian Literary Studies* 26 (2011): 1–5.

Davis, Kathleen. *Periodization and Sovereignty: How Ideas of Feudalism and Secularization Govern the Politics of Time* (Philadelphia: University of Pennsylvania Press, 2008).

Davis, Kathleen, and Nadia Altschul (eds.) *Medievalisms and the Postcolonial World: The Idea of 'the Middle Ages' outside Europe* (Baltimore, MD: Johns Hopkins University Press, 2009).

Delgado, Richard. 'Storytelling for Oppositionists and Others', in Richard Delgado and Jean Stefancic (eds.), *Critical Race Theory: The Cutting Edge*, 3rd ed. (Philadelphia, PA: Temple University Press, 2013), 71–80.

Deonn, Tracy. 'Every King Arthur Retelling Is Fanfic about Who Gets to Be Legendary', Tor.com. 23 March 2021. www.tor.com/2021/03/23/every-king-arthur-retelling-is-fanfic-about-who-gets-to-be-legendary.

Legendborn (London: Simon & Schuster, 2020).

DiVanna, Isabel. *Reconstructing the Middle Ages: Gaston Paris and the Development of Nineteenth-Century Medievalism* (Newcastle Upon Tyne: Cambridge Scholars Press, 2008).

Downes, Stephanie, and Helen Young. 'The Maiden Fair: Nineteenth-Century Medievalist Art and the Gendered Aesthetics of Whiteness in HBO's

Game of Thrones', *Postmedieval* 10 (2019): 219–35. https://doi.org/ 10.1057/s41280-019-00124-0.

Driver, Martha W., and Sid Ray (eds.) *The Medieval Hero on Screen: Representations from Beowulf to Buffy* (Jefferson, NC: McFarland, 2004).

Eco, Umberto. *Travels in Hyperreality* (San Diego, CA: Harvest Books, 1995).

El-Zein, Amira. *Islam, Arabs, and the Intelligent World of the Djinn* (Syracuse, NY: Syracuse University Press, 2009).

Ellard, Donna Beth. *Anglo-Saxon(ist) Pasts, postSaxon Futures* (New York: punctum books, 2019).

'Historical Hauntings: Coloniality, Decoloniality, and the Futures of Medieval Studies', *postmedieval* 10.2 (2019): 236–49. https://doi.org/ 10.1057/s41280-019-00128-w.

Elliott, Andrew B. R. *Medievalism, Politics and Mass Media: Appropriating the Middle Ages in the Twenty-First Century* (Cambridge: Boydell and Brewer, 2017).

'"Our Minds Are in the Gutter, but Some of Us Are Watching Starz . . .": Sex, Violence, and Dirty Medievalism', in Helen Young (ed.), *Fantasy and Science Fiction Medievalisms: From Isaac Asimov to 'A Game of Thrones'* (Amherst, NY: Cambria Press, 2015), 97–116.

Remaking the Middle Ages: The Methods of Cinema and History in Portraying the Medieval World (Jefferson, NC: McFarland, 2011).

Fimi, Dimitra. *Tolkien, Race, and Cultural History* (London: Palgrave Macmillan, 2009).

Finke, Laurie A., and Martin B. Shichtman. *King Arthur and the Myth of History* (Gainesville: University Press of Florida, 2002).

Finn, Kavita Mudan. 'Conversations in the Margins: Fannish Paratexts and Their Premodern Roots', *Journal of Fandom Studies* 5.2 (2017). www.ingentacon nect.com/content/intellect/jfs/2017/00000005/00000002/art00003.

Finn, Kavita Mudan, and Jessica McCall. 'Exit, Pursued by a Fan: Shakespeare, Fandom, and the Lure of the Alternate Universe', in Rob Conkie and Scott Maisano (eds.), *Shakespeare & Creative Criticism* (New York: Berghahn, 2018), 38–53.

Firchow, Peter E. 'The Politics of Fantasy: The Hobbit and Fascism', *Midwest Quarterly* 50.1 (2008): 15–31.

Fiske, John. *Understanding Popular Culture*, 2nd ed. (New York: Routledge, 2010).

Fitzpatrick, Kellyann. *Neomedievalism: Popular Culture and the Academy* (Cambridge: D. S. Brewer, 2019).

Ganim, John M. *Medievalism and Orientalism* (Basingstoke: Palgrave Macmillan, 2005).

Geary, Patrick. *The Myth of Nations: The Medieval Origins of Europe* (Princeton, NJ: Princeton University Press, 2002).

Hankins, Rebecca. 'Fictional Islam: A Literary Review and Comparative Essay on Islam in Science Fiction and Fantasy', *Foundation* 105 (2009): 73–92.

Hannam, Kevin, Mimi Sheller, and John Urry. 'Mobilities, Immobilities and Moorings', *Mobilities* 1.1 (2006): 1–22.

Hardy, Mat. 'The Crack of Dorne', in Lindsey Mantoan and Sara Brady (eds.), *Vying for the Iron Throne: Essays on Power, Gender, Death and Performance in HBO's Game of Thrones* (Jefferson, NC: McFarland, 2018), 16–27.

'The East Is Least: The Stereotypical Imagining of Essos in Game of Thrones', *Canadian Review of American Studies* 49.1 (2019): 26–45. https://doi.org/10.3138/cras.49.1.003.

'Games of Tropes: The Orientalist Tradition in the Works of G. R. R. Martin', *International Journal of Arts & Sciences* 8.1 (2015): 409–20.

'Godless Savages and Lockstep Legions: Examining Military Orientalism in *Game of Thrones*', *Journal of Asia-Pacific Pop Culture* 4.2 (2019): 192–212. https://doi.org/10.5325/jasiapacipopcult.4.2.0192.

Hartnett, Rachel M. '"The Silver Queen": US Imperialism and A Song of Ice and Fire', *The Journal of Popular Culture* 54.1 (2021): 146–64.

Harty, Kevin J. 'Introduction: "Save Us, O Lord, from the Fury of the Northmen"; or, "Do You Know What's in Your Wallet?"', in Kevin J. Harty (ed.), *The Vikings on Film: Essays on Depictions of the Nordic Middle Ages* (Jefferson, NC: McFarland, 2011), 3–7.

The Reel Middle Ages: American, Western and Eastern European, Middle Eastern and Asian Films about Medieval Europe (Jefferson, NC: McFarland, 1999).

Hendricks, Margo, 'Coloring the Past, Considerations on Our Future: RaceB4Race', *New Literary History* 52.3/4 (2021): 365–84.

Heng, Geraldine. 'An Arthurian Empire of Magic, and Its Discontents: An Afterword', *Arthuriana* 31.2 (2021): 124–38.

'Early Globalities, and Its Questions, Objectives, and Methods: An Inquiry into the State of Theory and Critique', *Exemplaria* 26.2–3 (2014): 234–53.

'The Global Middle Ages: An Experiment in Collaborative Humanities, or Imagining the World, 500–1500 C.E', *English Language Notes* 47.1 (2009): 205–16.

The Invention of Race in the European Middle Ages (Cambridge: Cambridge University Press, 2018).

'Romancing the Portal: MappaMundi and the Global Middle Ages', in Jennifer E. Boyle and Helen J. Burgess (eds.), *The Routledge Companion to Digital Medieval Literature* (Routledge, 2017), 31–46.

Heng, Geraldine, and Lynn Ramey. 'Early Globalities, Global Literatures: Introducing a Special Issue on the Global Middle Ages', *Literature Compass* 11.7 (2014): 389–94. https://doi.org/10.1111/lic3.12156.

Hirst, Michael. *Vikings* 4.4 'Yol', dir. Helen Shaver (History Channel, 2016).

Vikings 6.1 'New Beginnings', dir. Steve Saint Leger (History Channel, 2019).

Vikings 6.19 'The Lord Giveth', dir. Steve Saint Leger (History Channel, 2020).

Vikings 6.20 'The Last Act', dir. Steve Saint Leger (History Channel, 2020).

hooks, bell. *Outlaw Culture: Resisting Representations* (New York: Routledge, 1994).

Horsman, Reginald. *Race and Manifest Destiny: The Origins of American Racial Anglo-Saxonism* (Cambridge, MA: Harvard University Press, 1986).

Howey, Ann. *Rewriting the Women of Camelot: Arthurian Popular Fiction and Feminism* (Westport, CT: Greenwood, 2001).

Hsy, Jonathan. *Antiracist Medievalisms: From 'Yellow Peril' to Black Lives Matter* (Leeds: ARC Humanities, 2021).

Huysmans, Jef. *The Politics of Insecurity: Fear, Migration and Asylum in the EU* (Abingdon: Routledge, 2006).

Ingham, Patricia Clare. *Sovereign Fantasies: Arthurian Romance and the Making of Britain* (Philadelphia: University of Pennsylvania Press, 2001).

Innes, Paul. *Epic* (New York: Taylor & Francis, 2013).

James, Edward. 'Epics in Three Parts', *Journal of the Fantastic in the Arts* 29.1 (2019): 7–17.

James, McDonald. 'S. A. Chakraborty', *Kirkus*, 15 November 2017. www .kirkusreviews.com/news-and-features/articles/s-chakraborty.

Jamison, Carol Parrish. 'A Girl Is Arya: Acting and the Power of Performance', in Lindsey Mantoan and Sara Brady (eds.), *Vying for the Iron Throne: Essays on Power, Gender, Death and Performance in HBO's* Game of Thrones (Jefferson, NC: McFarland, 2018), 159–70.

Jemisin, N. K. 'Identity Should Always Be Part of the Gameplay', *Epiphany 2.0*, 2 August 2012. http://nkjemisin.com/2012/08/identity-should-always-be-part-of-the-gameplay.

Kao, Wan-Chuan. 'The Fragile Giant', *Arthuriana* 31.2 (2021): 9–39.

Kaplan, Merrill. 'The State of Vinland', in Nicholas Mayelan and Lukas Rosli (eds.), *Old Norse Myths As Political Ideologies: Critical Studies in the Appropriation of Medieval Narratives* (Turnhout: Brepols, 2020), 233–49.

Karkov, Catherine E., Anna Kłosowska, and Vincent W. J. van Gerven Oei (eds.). *Disturbing Times: Medieval Pasts, Reimagined Futures.* (New York: punctum books, 2020).

Keene, Bryan C. (ed.). *Toward a Global Middle Ages: Encountering the World through Illuminated Manuscripts* (Los Angeles: Getty Publications, 2019).

Khan, Ausma Zehanat. 'The Once and Future Qadi', in Swapna Krishna and Jenn Northington (eds.), *Sword Stone Table: Old Legends, New Voices* (New York: Vintage, 2021, 3–37.

Kim, Dorothy. 'Teaching Medieval Studies in a Time of White Supremacy', *In The Middle*, 28 August 2017, www.inthemedievalmiddle.com/2017/08/teaching-medieval-studies-in-time-of.html.

Kinoshita, Sharon. *Medieval Boundaries: Rethinking Difference in Old French Literature* (Pittsburgh: University of Pennsylvania Press, 2006)

Knight, Stephen. *Arthurian Literature and Society* (London: Macmillan, 1983).
  Reading Robin Hood: Content, Form and Reception in the Outlaw Myth (Machester: Manchester University Press, 2015).

Kolodny, Annette. *In Search of First Contact: The Vikings of Vinland, the Peoples of the Dawnland, and the Anglo-American Anxiety of Discovery* (Durham, NC: Duke University Press, 2012).

Krebs, Christopher B. *A Most Dangerous Book: Tacitus's Germania from the Roman Empire to the Third Reich* (New York: Norton, 2011).

Krishna, Swapna. 'S. A. Chakraborty's The City of Bress Started Out As History Fan Fiction', SyfyWire, 15 November 2017.
  Note: Unfortunately the link to the interview is dead as of spring 2022, but the interviewer (Swapna Krishna) kindly granted us access to an original transcript.

Krishna, Swapna, and Jenn Northington (eds.). *Sword Stone Table: Old Legends, New Voices* (New York: Vintage, 2021).

Lampert-Weissig, Lisa. *Medieval Literature and Postcolonial Studies* (Edinburgh: Edinburgh University Press, 2010).

Larrington, Carolyne. *Winter Is Coming: The Medieval World of* Game of Thrones (London: I. B. Tauris, 2015).

Lavezzo, Kathy. 'Whiteness, Medievalism, Immigration: Rethinking Tolkien through Stuart Hall', *postmedieval* 12 (2021): 21–59.

Lomuto, Sierra. 'Becoming Postmedieval: The Stakes of the Global Middle Ages', *postmedieval* 11.4(2020): 503–12. https://doi.org/10.1057/s41280-020-00198-1.

Lutz, John. 'Myth Understandings: First Contact, Over and Over Again', in John Lutz (ed.), *Myth and Memory: Rethinking Stories of Indigenous–European Contact* (Vancouver, BC: University of British Columbia Press, 2007), 1–15.

Lynch, Andrew. 'Post-colonial Studies', in Leah Tether and Johnny McFayden (eds.), *Handbook of Arthurian Romance* (Berlin: De Gruyter, 2017), 307–20.

Marshall, David W. *Mass Market Medieval: Essays on the Middle Ages in Popular Culture* (Jefferson, NC: McFarland, 2007).

'Neomedievalism, Identification, and the Haze of Medievalism', *Studies in Medievalism* 20 (2011): 21–34.

Martin, George R. R. *A Dance with Dragons* (New York: Bantam, 2011).

A Feast for Crows (New York: Bantam, 2005).

Fire & Blood: A History of House Targaryen (New York: Bantam, 2018).

A Game of Thrones: The First Book of A Song of Ice and Fire (New York: Bantam, 1996).

'We're Number One … ', Not a Blog, 6 July 2013. https://grrm.livejournal .com/326474.html?thread=17886026#t17886026.

Martin, George R. R., Elio M. García, and Linda Antonsson. *The World of Ice and Fire* (London: HarperCollins, 2014).

Martin, Richard P. 'Epic As Genre', in John Miles Foley (ed.), *A Companion to Ancient Epic* (Oxford: Blackwell, 2008), 9–19.

Matthews, David. *Medievalism: A Critical History* (Cambridge: D. S. Brewer, 2015).

McKittrick, Katherine. *Demonic Grounds: Black Women and the Cartographies of Struggle* (Minneapolis: University of Minnesota Press, 2006).

Mitchell-Smith, Ilan. 'The United Princesses of America: Ethnic Diversity and Cultural Purity in Disney's Medieval Past', in Tison Pugh and Susan Aronstein (eds.), *The Disney Middle Ages: A Fairy-Tale and Fantasy Past* (New York: Palgrave Macmillan, 2012), 209–24.

Miyashiro, Adam. 'Decolonizing Anglo-Saxon Studies: A Response to ISAS in Honolulu', In the Middle, 28 July 2017, www.inthemedievalmiddle.com/ 2017/07/decolonizing-anglo-saxon-studies.html.

'Our Deeper Past: Race, Settler Colonialism, and Medieval Heritage Politics', *Literature Compass* 16.9–10 (2019): 1–11. https://doi.org/10.1111/lic3.12550.

Momma, Haruko. 'Medievalism–Colonialism–Orientalism: Japan's Modern Identity in Natsume Sōseki's *Maboroshi No Tate* and *Kairo-kō*', in Kathleen Davis and Nadia R. Altschul (eds.), *Medievalisms in the Postcolonial World: The Idea of 'the Middle Ages' Outside Europe* (Baltimore, MD: Johns Hopkins University Press, 2009), 141–73.

Monteiro, Lyra D. 'Power Structures: White Columns, White Marble, White Supremacy', *Intersectionist*, 27 October 2020. https://intersectionist .medium.com/american-power-structures-white-columns-white-marble- white-supremacy-d43aa091b5f9.

Moreton-Robinson, Aileen. *The White Possessive: Property, Power, and Indigenous Sovereignty* (Minneapolis: University of Minnesota Press, 2015).

Nielsen, E. J. 'Christine de Pizan's *The Book of the City of Ladies* As Reclamatory Fan Work', *Transformative Works and Cultures* 6 (2017). https://doi.org/10.3983/twc.2017.01032.

Obertino, J. 'Barbarians and Imperialism in Tacitus and *The Lord of the Rings*', *Tolkien Studies* 3 (2006): 117–31.

Olomi, Ali A. *Head on History*. Podcast. 2017–present.

Ong, Aiwah. *Neoliberalism As Exception: Mutations in Citizenship and Sovereignty* (Durham, NC: Duke University Press, 2006).

Otaño Gracia, Nahir. 'Broken Dreams: Medievalism, Mulataje, and Mestizaje in the Work of Alejandro Tapia y Rivera', *Arthuriana* 31.2 (2021): 77–107. https://doi.org/10.1016/S0262-4079(18)30530-X.

Painter, Nell Irvin. *The History of White People* (New York: Norton, 2010).

Palmer-Patel, C. *The Shape of Fantasy: Investigating the Structure of American Heroic Epic Fantasy* (New York: Routledge, 2019).

Pask, Kevin. 'Resistance to Teaching', *Australian Humanities Review* 68.5 (May 2021): 38–43.

'Presidential Proclamation – Leif Erikson Day, 2016 | Whitehouse.Gov'. https://obamawhitehouse.archives.gov/the-press-office/2016/10/07/presidential-proclamation-leif-erikson-day-2016.

Qitsualik-Tinsley, Rachel, and Sean Qitsualik-Tinsley. *Skraelings: Clashes in the Old Arctic* (Iqaluit, Nunavut: Inhabit Media, 2014).

Rajabzadeh, Shokoofeh. 'The Depoliticized Saracen and Muslim Erasure', *Literature Compass* 16.9–10 (2019), 1–8. https://doi.org/10.1111/lic3.12548.

Rambaran-Olm, Mary. 'Anglo-Saxon Studies, Academia and White Supremacy', *Medium.com*, 27 June 2018, https://medium.com/@mrambaranolm/anglo-saxon-studies-academia-and-white-supremacy-17c87b360bf3.

'Sounds about White: Review of Mattew Gabriele and David M. Perry's *The Bright Ages*', *Medium.com*, 24 April 2022. https://mrambaranolm.medium.com/sounds-about-white-333d0c0fd201.

'A Wrinkle in Medieval Time: Ironing out Issues Regarding Race, Temporality, and the Early English', *New Literary History* 52.3/4 (2021): 385–406.

Rambaran-Olm, Mary, M. Breann Leake, and Micah James Goodrich. 'Medieval Studies: The Stakes of the Field', *postmedieval* 11.4 (2020): 356–70. https://doi.org/10.1057/s41280-020-00205-5.

Rambaran-Olm, Mary, and Erik Wade. 'The Many Myths of the Term "Anglo-Saxon"', Smithsonianmag.com, 14 July 2021. www.smithsonianmag.com/history/many-myths-term-anglo-saxon-180978169.

Richards, Julian D. *Vikings: A Very Short Introduction* (Oxford: Oxford University Press, 2005).

Rix, Robert W. 'Romancing Scandinavia: Relocating Chivalry and Romance in Eighteenth-Century Britain', *European Romantic Review* 20.1 (2009): 3–20.

Said, Edward. *Orientalism*. Reprint 1 (London: Penguin Books, 1995).

Schine, Rachel. 'Conceiving the Pre-modern Black Arab Hero: On the Gendered Production of Racial Difference in *Sīrat al-amīrah dhāt al-himmah*', *Journal of Arabic Literature* 48 (2017): 298 326.

— *Teaching Module: Race and Blackness in Early Islamic Thought*. Center for Religion & the Human. Indiana University. https://crh.indiana.edu/teaching-religion-in-public/engaging-religion/teaching-modules/schine-module.html.

Shannon, Samantha. 'Damsels Undistressed', Boundless, 2020. https://unbound.com/boundless/2020/03/31/samantha-shannon-retellings.

— *The Priory of the Orange Tree*. London: Bloomsbury, 2019.

Shaver, Helen. *Yol*. History Channel, 2016.

Sheller, Mimi, and John Urry. 'The New Mobilities Paradigm', *Environment and Planning A: Economy and Space* 38.2 (2006): 207–26. https://doi.org/10.1068/a37268.

Shichtman, Martin, and Laurie A. Finke. 'Exegetical History: Nazis at the Round Table', *postmedieval* 5.3 (2014): 278–94.

Shippey, T. A. *The Road to Middle Earth* (London: HarperCollins, 1982).

Shutters, Lyn. 'Viking through the Eyes of an Arab Ethnographer: Constructions of the Other in *The 13th Warrior*', in Lynn Ramey and Tison Pugh (eds.), *Race, Class, and Gender in 'Medieval' Cinema* (New York: Palgrave Macmillan, 2007), 75–89.

Skeggs, Beverly. *Class, Self, Culture* (New York: Routledge, 2004).

Sklar, Elizabeth. 'Call of the Wild: Culture Shock and Viking Masculinities in *The 13th Warrior*', in Kevin J. Harty (ed.), *The Vikings on Film: Essays on Depictions of the Nordic Middle Ages* (Jefferson, NC: McFarland, 2011), 121–34.

Sklar, Elizabeth, and Donald L. Hoffman, eds. *King Arthur in Popular Culture* (Jefferson, NC: McFarland, 2007).

Steinberg, Theodore. *Twentieth-Century Epic Novels* (Newark: University of Delaware Press, 2005).

Sturtevant, Paul B. 'Based on a True History? The Impact of Popular 'Medieval Film' on the Public Understanding of the Middle Ages', University of Leeds, 2010.

Sundmark, Bjorn. 'Wayward Warriors: The Viking Motif in Swedish and English Children's Literature', *Children's Literature in Education* 45 (2014): 197–210. https://doi.org/10.1007/s10583-013-9210-y.

Swank, Kris. 'The Arabian Nights in 21st-Century Fantasy Fiction', in Helen Young (ed.), *Fantasy and Science Fiction Medievalisms: From Isaac Asimov to 'A Game of Thrones'* (Amherst: Cambria Press, 2015), 163–95.

Szeman, Imre, and Susie O'Brien. *Popular Culture: A User's Guide. The Eloquence of the Vulgar* (Oxford: Wiley, 2017).

Thomas, Ebony Elizabeth. *The Dark Fantastic: Race and the Imagination from Harry Potter to* The Hunger Games (New York: New York University Press, 2019).

Thompson, Ayanna. 'Practicing a Theory/Theorizing a Practice: An Introduction to Shakespearean Colorblind Casting', in Ayanna Thompson (ed.), *Colorblind Shakespeare: New Perspectives on Race and Performance* (London: Routledge, 2006), 1–24.

Tolhurst, Fiona. 'Helping Girls to Be Heroic? Some Recent Arthurian Fiction for Young Adults', *Arthuriana* 22.3 (2012): 69–90.

Tolkien, J. R. R. *The Return of the King* (London: HarperCollins, 2007).

The Letters of J. R. R. Tolkien, ed. Humphrey Carpenter (London: HarperCollins, 2012).

Trombetta, Sadie. 'If You Love "Game Of Thrones," Don't Miss The Feminist Epic "The Priory Of The Orange Tree"', *Bustle*, 27 February 2019. www .bustle.com/p/the-priory-of-the-orange-tree-is-epic-feminist-fantasy-perfect-for-fans-of-game-of-thrones-16164155.

Utz, Richard. 'A Moveable Feast: Repositionings of "The Medieval" in Medieval Studies, Medievalism, and Neomedievalism', in Carol L. Robinson and Pamela Clements (eds.), *Neomedievalism in the Media* (Lewiston: Edwin Mellen, 2012), i–v.

Vernon, Matthew X. *The Black Middle Ages: Race and the Construction of the Middle Ages* (New York: Palgrave Macmilllan, 2018).

Vishnuvajjala, Usha. 'Gender, Adaptation, and the Future in David Lowery's *The Green Knight*', *The Sundial* (ACMRS Arizona), 3 May 2022. https:// medium.com/the-sundial-acmrs/gender-adaptation-and-the-future-in-david-lowerys-the-green-knight-7b967376c92f.

Warren, Michelle R. *Creole Medievalism: Colonial France and Joseph Bédier's Middle Ages* (Minneapolis: University of Minnesota Press, 2011).

'Making Contact: Postcolonial Perspectives through Geoffrey of Monmouth's Historia Regum Britannie', *Arthuriana* 8.4 (1998): 115–34. https://doi.org/ 10.1353/art.1988.0009.

Wawn, Andrew. *The Vikings and the Victorians: Inventing the Old North in Nineteenth-Century Britain* (Cambridge: D. S. Brewer, 2000).

Williams, Rebecca. 'Fan Tourism and Pilgrimage', in Melissa A. Click and Suzanne Scott (eds.), *The Routledge Companion to Media Fandom* (London: Routledge, 2017), 98–106.

Wilson, Anna. 'Full-Body Reading', *Aeon*, 10 November 2016. https://aeon.co/essays/how-a-medieval-mystic-was-the-first-creator-of-fanfiction.

Wilton, David. 'What Do We Mean By *Anglo-Saxon*? Pre-Conquest to the Present', *Journal of English and Germanic Philology* 119.4 (2020): 425–54. https://doi.org/10.5406/jenglgermphil.119.4.0425.

Winthrop-Young, Geoffrey. 'The Rise and Fall of Norse America: Vikings, Vinland and Alternate History', *Extrapolation: A Journal of Science Fiction and Fantasy* 43.2 (2002): 188–203.

Wymer, Kathryn. 'A Quest for the Black Knight: Casting People of Color in Arthurian Film and Television', *The Year's Work in Medievalism* 27 (2012) https://ywim.net/previous-issues/ywim-27-2012/.

Xie, Shabob. 'Rethinking the Identity of Cultural Otherness: The Discourse of Difference as Unfinished Project', in Roderick McGillis (ed.), *Voices of the Other: Children's Literature in the Postcolonial Context* (London: Routledge, 1999), 1–16.

Young, Helen. 'A Decolonizing Medieval Studies? Temporality and Sovereignty', *English Language Notes* 58.2 (2020): 50–63. https://doi.org/10.1215/00138282-8557910.

'Diversity and Difference: Cosmopolitanism and The Lord of the Rings', *Journal of the Fantastic in the Arts* 21.3 (2010): 351–65.

Young, Helen, ed. *Fantasy and Science Fiction Medievalisms: From Isaac Asimov to 'A Game of Thrones'* (Amherst: Cambria Press, 2015).

'Place and Time: Medievalism and Making Race', *The Year's Work in Medievalism* 28 (2013): np. https://sites.google.com/site/theyearsworkin medievalism/all-issues/28-2013.

'Race, Medievalism and the Eighteenth-Century Gothic Turn', *Postmedieval* 11, no. 4 (2020): 468–75. https://doi.org/10.1057/s41280-020-00203-7.

Race and Popular Fantasy Literature: Habits of Whiteness. (London: Routledge, 2016).

Young, Helen, ed. *The Middle Ages in Popular Culture: Medievalism, Genre, and Identity* (Amherst: Cambria Press, 2015).

'Thomas Percy's Racialization of the European Middle Ages', *Literature Compass* 16.9–10 (2019): 1–11. https://doi.org/10.1111/lic3.12543.

Young, Robert J. C. *The Idea of English Ethnicity* (Malden, MA: Blackwell, 2008).

Acknowledgements

To produce a book under normal circumstances requires a village; to produce one during a pandemic has changed that word's meaning. The authors wish to thank, first and foremost, Geraldine Heng and Susan Noakes for inviting us to join this excellent and much-needed series; but also Sabina Rahman, Helen's tireless research assistant; the authors, journalists, and fan artists who gave us their insights and feedback; our partners, for taking on extra parenting duties so we could write even during lockdowns when all the day cares were closed; and the vibrant medievalist, early modernist, pop culture studies, and fan communities on social media whose labour and brilliance we hope to highlight here.

Except for Kavita's dogs (RIP Nigel, excluded for the final time) and Helen's cat. They contributed nothing but excess fur.

Cambridge Elements ≡

The Global Middle Ages

Geraldine Heng

University of Texas at Austin

Geraldine Heng is Perceval Professor of English and Comparative Literature at the University of Texas, Austin. She is the author of *The Invention of Race In the European Middle Ages* (2018) and *England and the Jews: How Religion and Violence Created the First Racial State in the West* (2018), both published by Cambridge University Press, as well as *Empire of Magic: Medieval Romance and the Politics of Cultural Fantasy* (2003, Columbia). She is the editor of *Teaching the Global Middle Ages* (2022, MLA), coedits the University of Pennsylvania Press series, RaceB4Race: Critical Studies of the Premodern, and is working on a new book, Early Globalisms: The Interconnected World, 500–1500 CE. Originally from Singapore, Heng is a Fellow of the Medieval Academy of America, a member of the Medievalists of Color, and Founder and Co-director, with Susan Noakes, of the Global Middle Ages Project: www.globalmiddleages.org.

Susan Noakes

University of Minnesota, Twin Cities

Susan Noakes is Professor and Chair of French and Italian at the University of Minnesota, Twin Cities. From 2002 to 2008 she was Director of the Center for Medieval Studies; she has also served as Director of Italian Studies, Director of the Center for Advanced Feminist Studies, and Associate Dean for Faculty in the College of Liberal Arts. Her publications include *The Comparative Perspective on Literature: Essays in Theory and Practice* (co-edited with Clayton Koelb, Cornell, 1988) and *Timely Reading: Between Exegesis and Interpretation* (Cornell, 1988), along with many articles and critical editions in several areas of French, Italian, and neo-Latin Studies. She is the Founder and Co-director, with Geraldine Heng, of the Global Middle Ages Project: www.globalmiddleages.org.

About the Series

Elements in the Global Middle Ages is a series of concise studies that introduce researchers and instructors to an uncentered, interconnected world, c. 500–1500 CE. Individual Elements focus on the globe's geographic zones, its natural and built environments, its cultures, societies, arts, technologies, peoples, ecosystems, and lifeworlds.

Cambridge Elements ≡

The Global Middle Ages

Elements in the Series

The Global Middle Ages: An Introduction
Geraldine Heng

The Market in Poetry in the Persian World
Shahzad Bashir

Oceania, 800-1800CE: A Millennium of Interactions in a Sea of Islands
James L. Flexner

Cahokia and the North American Worlds
Sarah E. Baires

Eurasian Musical Journeys: Five Tales
Gabriela Currie and Lars Christensen

Global Medievalism: An Introduction
Helen Young and Kavita Mudan Finn

A full series listing is available at: www.cambridge.org/EGMA

Printed in the United States
by Baker & Taylor Publisher Services

Printed in the United States
by Baker & Taylor Publisher Services